Apostasy, destruction and hope

Apostasy, destruction and hope

2 Kings simply explained

Roger Ellsworth

 **EVANGELICAL PRESS**

EVANGELICAL PRESS
Faverdale North, Darlington, DL3 0PH, England

e-mail: sales@evangelicalpress.org

Evangelical Press USA
P. O. Box 825, Webster, New York 14580, USA

e-mail: usa.sales@evangelicalpress.org

web: http://www.evangelicalpress.org

First published 2002
Reprinted 2005

British Library Cataloguing in Publication Data available

ISBN-13 978-0-85234-510-8   ISBN 0 85234 510 0

Printed and bound in Great Britain by Creative Print & Design Wales, Ebbw Vale

The following pages are dedicated to
Todd and Stephanie Greer
and their children,
Jacob, Elijah, Holly and Olivia.

Acknowledgements

I am deeply grateful to the saints of Immanuel Baptist Church who gladly received much of this material in sermon form. Special thanks go to my secretary, Laura Simmons, for bringing her wonderful skills and trademark enthusiasm to this project, as well as to my wife Sylvia for her encouragement and assistance.

As always, I am delighted to be associated with Evangelical Press and appreciate more than words can convey the kind assistance of her editors and reviewers.

Roger Ellsworth

Contents

Introduction

What makes 2 Kings a suitable topic of study? Does it really have anything of value to say to us? The mere suggestion may seem ludicrous to some. How could a book so far removed from our own time possibly contain anything of importance for us? We shall soon see. But we must first put in place some general information.

This book was not written as mere history. It is history as interpreted by a prophet (some say Jeremiah was the author). 2 Kings is essentially proclamation. It is the author preaching to his readers about some crucial truths. The *Personal Study Bible* well says, 'The accounts do not attempt to give a comprehensive record of all events during the years covered. Rather, the purpose is to give a theological analysis of those particular persons or events which had a negative or positive effect upon the eventual outcome of the nations... The basis for that analysis is obedience or disobedience to the law of God (17:13-23; 21:10-16), especially as seen in Deuteronomy.'[1]

The same source offers this note: '... the author uses Israel's history to illustrate the two paths in life between which all of us must choose. The one pursues God in heart as well as in religious forms, and pleases him. The other fails to obey God because of a lack of devotion.'[2]

The readers

The primary readership

The author of 2 Kings wrote primarily for his own people who had been taken captive. 2 Kings is the book of downfalls, or captivities. As it opens we find the people of God divided into two kingdoms: Israel and Judah. Neither kingdom was to last. The seventeenth chapter tells us about the kingdom of Israel being taken captive by the Assyrians. One verse neatly encapsulates this: 'Therefore the LORD was very angry with Israel, and removed them from his sight; there was none left but the tribe of Judah alone' (17:18).

The closing chapters tell us about the kingdom of Judah being taken captive by the Babylonians. This event is summarized in the following words: 'And the LORD said, "I will also remove Judah from my sight, as I have removed Israel, and will cast off this city Jerusalem which I have chosen..."' (23:27).

Two kingdoms — both taken into captivity! It is impossible for us adequately to comprehend how devastating this was for the Israelites. They needed help, and the author of 2 Kings provided it for them. He wrote to explain why the exile had taken place, to urge them to guard against dangers incurred while they were in captivity and to give them hope for the future.

A secondary readership

The emphasis given by the author to the schools of the prophets, which he designates as the 'sons of the prophets' (2:3,5,15; 4:1,38; 6:1), suggests that he had in mind a special group of readers within his larger readership, namely, the prophets of

God. We know that there were prophets among the people during their captivity in Babylon (Ezekiel, Daniel) and prophets after the exile (Haggai, Malachi, Zechariah, Zephaniah).

While there can be no doubt that the author's accounts about the prophets had meaning for all his readers, we may rest assured that they had special significance for the prophets of God. As they read the details of the ways in which God proved himself sufficient for his prophets in a time of militant and seemingly invincible paganism, they would have found themselves strengthened for the daunting challenges of both the exile and the post-exilic era. And, of course, every succeeding generation of godly ministers has been much encouraged by looking to these same sections of 2 Kings.

The reasons for their captivity

1. Idolatry

One of the principal reasons for the exile was the widespread and rampant idolatry of both Israel and Judah.

The people of these kingdoms were in a unique covenant relationship with God. God had called them unto himself as his special people and had given them the law of Moses by which to govern their lives. The essence of this law was the Ten Commandments (Exod. 20:1-17), and the very first of these commandments said, 'You shall have no other gods before me' (Exod. 20:3). The second commandment said, 'You shall not make for yourself a carved image — any likeness of anything that is in heaven above, or that is in the earth beneath, or that is in the water under the earth; you shall not bow down to them nor serve them. For I, the LORD your God, am a jealous God...' (Exod. 20:4-5). There were plenty of sins committed in both Israel and Judah before they were taken into captivity, but the one sin that provoked the Lord more than any other was idolatry.

When the nation of Israel split into the two kingdoms, Israel and Judah, idolatry immediately became rampant in the former. Jeroboam set up calves at Bethel and Dan (1 Kings 12:25-33). Then Ahab came along and plunged the nation into the worship of Baal on an unprecedented scale (1 Kings 16:30-33).

The author of 2 Kings summarizes Israel's fall into idolatry in this way: 'So they left all the commandments of the LORD their God, made for themselves a moulded image and two calves, made a wooden image and worshipped all the host of heaven, and served Baal. And they caused their sons and daughters to pass through the fire, practised witchcraft and soothsaying, and sold themselves to do evil in the sight of the LORD, to provoke him to anger' (17:16-17). Judah, which was ruled by the house of David, practised idolatry as well, especially during the reign of the wicked Manasseh (21:1-12; 22:16-17; 23:26).

We can disregard the message of 2 Kings when we are no longer inclined to practise idolatry. But we know that it is an ongoing and ever-present danger. We who know the Lord can give to other things the allegiance that belongs to him alone. When we do we are guilty of idolatry.

2. Refusal to heed the Word of God

The author forcefully makes this point in these words: 'Yet the LORD testified against Israel and against Judah, by all of his prophets, every seer, saying, "Turn from your evil ways, and keep my commandments and my statutes, according to all the law which I commanded your fathers, and which I sent to you by my servants the prophets." Nevertheless they would not hear, but stiffened their necks, like the necks of their fathers, who did not believe in the LORD their God. And they rejected his statutes and his covenant that he had made with their fathers, and his testimonies which he had testified against them...' (17:13-15).

The Word of God occupies centre stage in 2 Kings. It is the force that drives human history. We do not have prophets today, but the Word of God still sounds out. It calls us back, as it did God's people in Old Testament times, from our idolatries to love and serve the true and living God. It assures us of his forgiveness when we turn back to him with all our hearts. It warns us of his chastisement if we refuse to repent. How blessed we are to have the precious, holy Word of God!

And yet it is not enough simply to possess it. It is not enough even to read it or to hear it taught or preached. We must read it and hear it with a warm and welcoming reception. The author of Hebrews warned his readers about the terrible danger of being 'dull of hearing' (Heb. 5:11).

3. God's faithfulness

A third reason for their captivity might come as somewhat of a surprise. The exile seemed to prove that God had completely cast off his people, that he was unfaithful to them. The truth is that it proved exactly the opposite. They were in captivity because God was faithful to his promises.

Before the people of Israel ever occupied the land of Canaan, the Lord gave them this solemn warning: 'But if your heart turns away so that you do not hear, and are drawn away, and worship other gods and serve them, I announce to you today that you shall surely perish; you shall not prolong your days in the land which you cross over the Jordan to go in and possess' (Deut. 30:17-18). It should be noted that this warning came after others of a similar nature (Deut. 28:37,49-50,64). The captivity, then, proved the faithfulness of God!

A danger posed by captivity

The books of the Kings were also intended to deal with a challenge that their readers (exiles in Babylon) were currently facing, namely, to attempt to synthesize or blend their faith in God with the religious beliefs and practices of Babylon. The book of Daniel gives gripping testimony to this reality. Daniel and his friends were not pressurized to abandon their faith completely, but rather to make room alongside it for the worship of Babylon's gods. Time after time, Daniel and his fellow-captives refused (Dan. 1:3-16; 3:1-30; 6:1-28).

The captives in Babylon must have found themselves caught in a vice on this matter. The seductive allure of Babylon's charms and her political pressure were intense. But, on the other hand, those captives who were thoughtful and discerning had to know they had lost everything and come to Babylon precisely because of their failure to stand against syncretism. They and their fathers had vainly imagined that they could blend the worship of God with the worship of idols, that such a blending did no dishonour to God but merely brought them up to date and in step with the other nations. Their attempted synthesis met with woeful failure. A synthesis is impossible when two gods claim the same ground, and since the God of Israel claimed all the ground, there was absolutely no place left for another god.

2 Kings was to serve as a sober reminder of the impossibility of combining a sovereign God with any other god and, in doing so, it had to stiffen the resolve of the captives in Babylon against trying another synthesis there. To put it bluntly, they were in captivity because of syncretism, and they were now to avoid it at all costs.

The book of 2 Kings is no dead letter. It challenges us vigorously at several points. On no issue does it challenge the modern-day church more than this one. Syncretism is the motto of the day, as pastors and churches scurry about to harmonize biblical faith with the latest trend. Armed with poll numbers, religious leaders tell us that we cannot expect the biblical religion to be accepted if we do not bring it up-to-date. So the modern church professes faith in God and runs after the gods of growth, psychology, entertainment and successful living techniques. Meanwhile the God of heaven reminds us that no one can serve two masters (Matt. 6:24). We may assure ourselves that we are really giving allegiance to God while we pursue these other concerns, but now, as in 2 Kings, God demands our all. That means we must not only believe and preach his message, but also do so in the ways that please and honour him.

Hope for the future

If 2 Kings were only about idolatry and captivity, it would make for sombre reading indeed. It is more than that. It is also a book of hope.

How the captives in Babylon needed that note! In addition to losing everything they held near and dear, they found themselves in a severe crisis of faith. God had made glorious promises to them. Judah was the nation from which the Messiah was to come. King David was to be his ancestor. The Messiah was to come to their glorious temple. And now the nation of Judah and the house of David were in faraway Babylon, and there was no temple at all. It seemed that all was lost. But it only seemed that way. The author of 2 Kings wrote to explain to his exiled people why the captivity had taken place and to assure them that God had not finished with them.

The same faithfulness of God that had caused them to go into captivity now gave the exiles hope for the future. We might say the same faithfulness that had worked against them in the past was now working on their behalf! The very God who had fulfilled his word in bringing judgement upon them could be trusted to fulfil his promises to restore them to their land and to send the Messiah.

King Jehoiachin of Judah was treated kindly by the King of Babylon (25:27-30). We might be inclined to read this as nothing more than a historical note of little significance, but it had to be much more than that to the captives. Their king, a descendant of David, was being sustained and nurtured in Babylon! Then the promise of the Messiah was not lost! In seeing to it that Jehoiachin was sustained, God was sustaining his promise. It often looked as if the Messianic line would be eliminated. In his battle with the Christ, Satan has always employed two strategies: either to destroy the Messianic line, and especially the house of David, or to use idolatry to corrupt the true faith in Israel. The note on which 2 Kings closes shows that up to that point Satan had failed. He would continue to fail. The Messiah would come, just as God had promised (Gen. 3:15), and would provide eternal salvation for his people.

The themes hammered home by 2 Kings are truths that we ourselves need. We must obey God's command to worship and serve him alone. We must always pay careful heed to his Word. We can, and must, trust his promises. With these things firmly in place, we can face an uncertain future with a clear sense of direction and with a deep peace.

1.
A war of words

Please read 2 Kings 1:1-18

2 Kings begins with a troubled king on the throne of Israel. In short, swift strokes the author informs us that Moab had rebelled against Israel (1:1) and the king, Ahaziah, had suffered a serious fall. This may seem to be a rather peculiar way to begin unless we remind ourselves that 1 and 2 Kings were originally one book. The division was for the sake of convenience and apparently without regard to a natural place to break the narrative.

The account of Ahaziah's reign begins in the closing verses of 1 Kings. It was a short but dreadful reign as he continued the idolatrous ways of his father Ahab (1 Kings 22:51-53). Suddenly the opening verses of 2 Kings make sense. We are intended to interpret the rebellion of Moab and Ahaziah's fall against the backdrop of Ahaziah's idolatry. The king continues the wicked ways of his father and he immediately encounters troubles on every side. Was that just coincidence? Many would say it was, but what follows in this chapter shows us that the living God was confronting Ahaziah and giving him the opportunity to break with his idols. Our coincidences are God's providences.

How gracious God is! He would have been justified in discharging Ahaziah into the eternal realm without so much as a single warning, but God continued to strive with him by sending him trouble.

And how did the king respond to his troubles? Did he regard them as kind messengers from the Lord God and turn from his sins? Verse 2 tells us that he responded to his sickness by sending messengers to enquire of Baal-Zebub, the god of Ekron, whether he would recover. (Because the name 'Baal-Zebub', which means 'lord of a fly', is rather unflattering, some think a God-fearing scribe may have changed it from 'Baal-Zebul', which means 'glorious Baal'.)

Ekron was the northernmost city in the land of the Philistines. Some suggest that Ahaziah sent to consult this particular Baal because of the god's well-known prowess in healing. But it could very well be that Ahaziah had to send to Ekron because of the effectiveness of the ministry of Elijah the prophet. Ronald S. Wallace writes, 'What happened at Carmel changed the religious balance of power in Israel. Public opinion moved decisively to the side of the old religion of the Covenant. Elijah became the dominant figure in the background of the nation's life, and the prophets of the Lord were free to speak his word, give counsel, and intervene in national affairs. Yet Baalism became a still-powerful underground movement and, as the Naboth affair showed (1 Kings 21), it continued for nearly a generation to do severe damage here and there to what was traditional to Israel's life.'[1]

Ahaziah's decision to consult with Baal presented the original readers with a message of sharp significance. It is a message of immense relevance for us as well. We can make this message stand out in bold relief by underscoring three phrases: 'Thus says the LORD ...' (1:4,6,16); 'The king has said ...' (1:9,11); and 'So Ahaziah died according to the word of the LORD' (1:17). These phrases take us to the heart of this chapter. What we have here is a war between conflicting words, with one word eventually triumphing over the other.

'Thus says the Lord ...'

The Lord had not finished striving with Ahaziah. As the messengers made their way to Baal-Zebub, Elijah the prophet confronted them with these words: **'Is it because there is no God in Israel that you are going to enquire of Baal-Zebub, the god of Ekron? Now therefore, thus says the Lord: "You shall not come down from the bed to which you have gone up, but you shall surely die"'** (1:3-4). In sending to Baal-Zebub, Ahaziah was attributing to Baal the power that belonged to God alone. His father Ahab had attributed the rains and the lightning to Baal, but God had used Elijah on Mount Carmel to show that it was he, and not Baal, who controlled the weather. Here God uses Elijah again to teach Ahaziah the same lesson. It is God alone who controls life and death. Ahaziah's crisis was deepened by Elijah's sudden intervention with the Word of God. Would Ahaziah now believe the Word of God and humble himself before it?

Ahaziah had spent his whole life ignoring God and worshipping idols, but he could not escape. He was in God's hands, not those of Baal-Zebub, and God had determined that he would die.

'The king has said ...'

If ever there was an individual who had reason to respect the Word of God, it was Ahaziah. He had first-hand knowledge of the Word of God being confirmed again and again. His father Ahab had disregarded the Word of God and gone after Baal, lock, stock and barrel. What happened? God sent Elijah to announce a severe famine on the land (1 Kings 17:1). Ahaziah knew that the famine had come upon the land just as Elijah had said, and he also knew that the famine had ended at the word of Elijah (1 Kings 18:1,41-45). In addition to that Ahaziah had seen Elijah's word fulfilled in the death of his father. Ahab had further violated the Word of God by unlawfully seizing the vineyard of Naboth. God responded to Ahab's sin by again sending Elijah with a message of devastating judgement. This time Elijah was to tell Ahab that dogs would lick his own blood where the dogs of Jezreel had licked the blood of Naboth (1 Kings 21:1-29; 22:37-38). Ahaziah knew that this prophecy had been fulfilled down to the last detail.

But Ahaziah was an apostate. He was one who had decisively rejected the truth of God. Enraged by the message of Elijah, he sent in succession three captains, each with a company of fifty men.

The first captain

The first captain approached Elijah with these words: **'Man of God, the king has said, "Come down!"'** (1:9).

We should not be impressed by his use of the term 'man of God' in addressing Elijah. It is evident that he employed this title with contempt and ridicule, and not with respect. What we have here is a man setting himself against God and his Word. Elijah had already spoken God's message to King Ahaziah, but this captain had no hesitation in pitting the king's word against God's word.

Elijah responded by saying, **'If I am a man of God, then let fire come down from heaven and consume you and your fifty men'** (1:10). Elijah's request was immediately honoured as **'fire came down from heaven'** (1:10) to consume the captain and his company.

The second captain

The second captain, undoubtedly knowing the fate of his predecessor, approached Elijah without the slightest trace of respect or fear. Indeed, he showed even more contempt for Elijah by adding the words: **'Come down quickly!'** (1:11). This captain wanted Elijah to know that he was not a man to be trifled with and that the prophet had better obey, and do so quickly, or face very unpleasant consequences. Elijah responded to this captain with the very same words he had used in reply to the first one, and this captain and his company were also consumed (1:12). More defiance led to more fire.

Centuries later the Lord Jesus Christ and his disciples entered a Samaritan village where the inhabitants had rejected them. James and John, thinking of Elijah's response to these captains, asked Jesus for permission to call fire down from heaven. But Jesus rebuked them: 'You do not know what manner of spirit you are of. For the Son of Man did not come to destroy men's lives but to save them' (Luke 9:55-56). Some take Jesus' words to mean that Elijah was wrong in calling down fire from heaven. But we cannot take this position because it was God who sent the fire. If Elijah was wrong to call for the fire, God did not have to send it.

We are faced, then, with this question: why was it appropriate for Elijah to call down fire and inappropriate for Jesus' disciples to do the same? The answer lies in the change of dispensation. Matthew Henry writes, 'Elijah was sent to display the terrors of the law, and to give proof of that, and to witness as a bold reprover against the idolatries and wickednesses of the court of Ahab, and it was agreeable enough to him to have his commission thus proved; but it is a dispensation of grace that is now to be introduced, to which such a terrible display of divine justice will not be at all agreeable.'[2]

The *MacArthur Study Bible* adds: 'Elijah was commissioned to a special ministry as a prophet in a theocracy, and it was his God-ordained task to confront an evil monarch [Ahab] who was attempting to usurp God's authority. Elijah was specifically authorized to measure out the reprisal of God's wrath.

Elijah acted with an authority comparable to that of modern civil authorities (cf. Rom. 13:4) — not in a capacity that parallels that of ministers of the gospel.'[3]

The third captain

The king's intense hatred for God and his defiance of God's Word are revealed by his sending yet another captain. But this captain had taken to heart what had happened to those who had preceded him. He came to Elijah with a meek and submissive spirit: **'And the third captain of fifty went up, and came and fell on his knees before Elijah, and pleaded with him, and said to him: "Man of God, please let my life and the life of these fifty servants of yours be precious in your sight"'** (1:13). His plea for mercy was heard and he and his company were spared.

Now this captain has a vital lesson to teach us — the way to avoid God's wrath is to stop showing contempt for his Word and beg for his mercy. Joseph Hall says, 'There is nothing to be gotten from God by strong hand, any thing by suit.'[4]

This third captain and his company also serve as happy reminders that individuals can heed the Word of God even while the whole of society around them is steadily drifting from it.

'So Ahaziah died according to the word of the LORD'

We cannot leave this chapter without considering how it all turned out. After hearing the plea of the third captain and a word from **'the angel of the LORD'** (1:14,15), Elijah went back to Ahaziah. The king had defied the Word of God, but he had not succeeded in silencing it or changing it in any way. Elijah repeated the message (1:16), and the account reaches its climax with these words: **'So Ahaziah died according to the word of the LORD which Elijah had spoken'** (1:17).

Joseph Hall summarizes Ahaziah's reign in this way: 'Wickedness shortens his reign; he had too much of Ahab and Jezebel, to expect the blessing, either of length or prosperity of government. As always in the other, so oft-times in this world, doth God testify his anger to wicked men. Some live long, that they may aggravate their judgement; others die soon, that they may hasten it.'[5]

The solemn account of Ahaziah and his two captains and their companies is yet another example of God using judgement in the temporal realm to warn of eternal judgement (see Luke 13:1-5). This account reminds us that our God is indeed 'a consuming fire' (Heb. 12:29) and that those who fight against him are destined to lose.

What this account teaches

1. For the captives in Babylon

It is not hard to see the significance of 2 Kings 1 for the captives in Babylon. It served as a pointed reminder of why they were there. Ahaziah's true illness was apostasy, and with that illness he was emblematic of both Israel and Judah and their illness. As he went after Baal, so both nations went after idols. As his devotion to Baal led to his destruction, so the devotion of Israel and Judah to idols led them to destruction.

But the application of this account went even further. The captives had the Word of God there in Babylon, and they were called to function on the basis of that Word. They were called to believe that its promises to them were still intact, that their nation would eventually be released from captivity and restored to their homeland and their Messiah would finally come. They were called to live in obedience to its precepts, yes, even there in Babylon.

But the Word of God was not the only message sounding in their ears. They also constantly heard the message of Babylonian culture and religion. This message urged them to abandon their faith in God and become Babylonian in their thinking and doing.

The message of 2 Kings 1 must have come as a powerful reminder to those captives in that Babylonian pressure-cooker that the two messages they were hearing were not equal. They had been very eager to disregard God's truth and believe the message of false prophets, a message that cried, 'Peace, peace!' (Jer. 6:14; 8:11). But their very presence in Babylon proved that God's Word had triumphed over the message of the false prophets, and there was, therefore, every reason to believe it would triumph over the Babylonian message.

2. For the church today

It is also not hard to see the significance of this chapter for the church today. The very same God who gave Ahaziah such a clear message has given his church a message to convey to her world. This message tells us that we are not mere earthbound creatures who cease to exist at death, but that we are destined to go out into eternity and meet him when life is over. He tells us that we are not by nature prepared for this meeting. He tells us that he is holy and that he demands that we be holy. He tells us that we are sinners and, as such, deserving of his condemnation. He tells us that he is a consuming fire, and that if we appear before him in our sins, we shall most certainly be consumed by his wrath.

What a frightening message! But there is more. God also tells us that he has prepared a way by which we can have our sins forgiven and be granted eternal life and eternal fellowship with him. That way is his Son, Jesus Christ. The Lord Jesus took unto himself our humanity, and in that humanity went to the cross and there endured the wrath of God in the stead of all those who believe.

Many disdain this message, just as Ahaz and his captains disdained the message of Elijah. As the church says, 'Thus says the Lord,' our secular age responds with 'Thus says the king'. In other words, our world responds to the message of the church with one of its own, a message that flatly denies that proclaimed by the church. The message of this world always sounds so very sweet and appealing. And the church all too often places herself in an impossible situation, one in which she tries to embrace both the message of God and that of the world. She takes out of God's message those things that are considered most objectionable, and she suddenly discovers in God's message those beliefs that her society most cherishes.

All the while 2 Kings 1 joins with other scriptures to thunder out this truth to the church: 'Thus says the king' never takes precedence over 'Thus says the Lord'. Those who forget this do so to their own shame. They may feel very proud of themselves now for being so up-to-date and sophisticated and for making the church more palatable to modern folk. But when in eternity they encounter the living God who is zealous for his truth, their folly will be horrendously apparent to themselves and to the watching universe. Those who struggle against the Lord's truth struggle in vain.

2.
Elijah goes home

Please read 2 Kings 2:1-18

This chapter brings us to the end of one ministry and the beginning of another. Elijah had served God faithfully, but now, in the sovereign design of God, it was time for him to give way to Elisha.

This was to be a transition like no other. Elijah was not to step off the stage through retirement or death. He was to be swept soul and body into heaven itself, a plan which the Lord had apparently revealed to some degree to Elijah, Elisha and the prophets at both Bethel (2:3) and Jericho (2:5).

What a tower of spiritual strength Elijah had been for Israel! He had faithfully and courageously stood for God in a critical and faith-sapping time. The well-being of God's cause often appeared to rest completely on him. What would become of that cause now that he was to be removed from the scene? It was important that Elijah's removal be accomplished in such a way as to give powerful testimony to the truth that the cause of God goes on even when he changes the instruments he employs to maintain it.

The prelude to the home-going: Elisha is tested (2:1-10)

The author begins by relating the details of Elijah's final journey. Beginning at Gilgal, he, accompanied by Elisha, made his way to Bethel and Jericho before crossing the Jordan river. Elijah's visits to Gilgal, Bethel and Jericho, where there were schools of prophets, must have been marked by deep emotion. The men in these schools would have wondered what lay ahead for them and the nation of Israel now that this spiritual colossus was about to be taken away. They must also have wondered if Elisha was ready to step into Elijah's role as God's primary spokesman and the leader of the prophets. It was a critical time. Baal-worship was still a threat, and the calf-worship instituted by Jeroboam at Bethel was still flourishing (1 Kings 12:25-30).

Such times demanded a strong leader for the people of God, the type of man who could boldly stand against the flood of idolatry and who could strengthen the faith of God's beleaguered people. Elijah had been such a leader, but now he was to be taken from them. What about Elisha? Was he up to the task?

Elisha's firm resolve

Such concerns would soon be put to rest. Elisha began by demonstrating that he was a man who had the firm resolve demanded by the times. When Elijah set out on his final journey he told Elisha to stay in Gilgal (2:1-2). Elisha refused and joined him on his trip to Bethel. The pattern was repeated when Elijah set out from Bethel and from Jericho (2:4,6).

Can we say we are people of firm resolve today? We need not expect the cause of the Lord to prosper and flourish unless we possess such resolve. The Lord's work is flagging today because there is a shortage of Christians with ironclad commitment. We desire to see the Lord's work flourish, but there is a world of difference between desire and determination. Only the latter will move the cause of God forward.

Elisha's rejection of melancholy counsel

Elisha also demonstrated that he would not be swayed by melancholy counsel. When he and Elijah were about to leave Bethel the prophets there said to him, **'Do you know that the LORD will take away your master from over you today?'** (2:3). When the two men were ready to leave Jericho the prophets there said the same thing to him (2:5). In each case, Elisha responded by saying, **'Yes, I know; keep silent!'** (2:3,5).

What was all this about? It seems that in each case the prophets were preparing to draw a depressing, melancholy conclusion from the fact that Elijah was about to be taken away, but Elisha refused to let them do so. He cut them off before they had a chance to go ahead with their litany of woes: 'What are we going to do after Elijah is gone? What will become of the cause of God now? All is lost!'

Elisha knew that something in this vein was coming and he refused to listen to it. In like manner, if we expect to be the type of people who are used by God to preserve his cause we must stop our ears against the kind of pessimism that makes our task seem hopeless and must instead fill our minds and hearts with the promises of Holy Scripture that the cause of God is going to triumph.

Elisha's desire for the power of God

Finally, when he and Elijah had crossed the Jordan and were alone, Elisha demonstrated that he was a man who was filled with fervent, intense yearning for the power of God. There Elijah asked him, **'What may I do for you, before I am taken away from you?'** (2:9).

What a great opportunity this was for Elisha! Elijah was giving him, as it were, a blank cheque, and all Elisha had to do was fill in the amount. If we really want to know where we are spiritually, we can put ourselves in his shoes for a moment. What would we ask from God if we could have anything at all?

Elisha made this his request: **'Please let a double portion of your spirit be upon me'** (2:9). In Israel the eldest son received a double portion of his father's inheritance (Deut. 21:17). By virtue of the special call he received into the prophetic office through Elijah (1 Kings 19:19-21), Elisha considered himself to be the first-born among the other prophets. In asking for a double portion of Elijah's spirit, Elisha was asking to be confirmed as the true successor and heir of Elijah.

Elisha's request reminds us that the whole nation of Israel was God's first-born son whom he had called out of Egypt (Exod. 4:22: Hosea 11:1). As such the nation was entitled to wonderful spiritual privileges, but the people were content to live beneath their privileges.

His request also points us forward to the Lord Jesus Christ who, as God's first-born and beloved Son, was also called out of Egypt (Matt. 2:15). Unlike Elisha, the Lord Jesus did not have to ask for a double portion of his Father's Spirit, because he had the Spirit of God resting upon him without measure (John 3:34).

Elisha was, then, a man of firm resolve who refused to listen to the counsel of hopelessness and a man who fervently desired the power and the Spirit of God. These are the very qualities we must possess if we are to be used by God in this hour. Let us even now take courage in the fact that God's cause is going to triumph, but let us also resolve to be the type of men and women God can use to preserve his cause on earth until that glorious day in heaven.

The home-going itself (2:11-12)

Shortly after crossing the Jordan, and while Elijah and Elisha were engaged in conversation, a chariot and horses of fire appeared and swept Elijah away. As Elisha beheld the awesome sight, he cried, **'My father, my father, the chariot of Israel and its horsemen!'** (2:12). Elisha said this because he understood that Elijah's godly ministry had been Israel's strength and her security.

Elijah's is the second and last instance of such a translation in Scripture. Enoch was the first (Gen. 5:24), but his translation, we assume, lacked the spectacular element of the chariot and horses of fire.

Elijah's translation abounds with comfort and consolation for the people of God. It is not recorded as some kind of spectacular display tacked onto the account of Elijah's life. God did not do this merely to amaze us.

Supremacy over Baal

First, by this translation God showed yet again his supremacy over Baal. Raymond B. Dillard writes, 'In ancient Canaan, Baal was known as "the Rider of the Clouds". He was a warlike weather deity. The billowing dark clouds of a storm were viewed as the battle chariot in which Baal rode, thundering forth his voice and carrying lightning as his spear.'[1]

Elijah's ministry was designed to show that the devotees of Baal were guilty of attributing to a non-god the prerogatives of the true God. Through the famine announced by Elijah,

God had shown that Baal could not send the life-giving rains (1 Kings 17:1). When rain did come it was made abundantly clear to the nation that it was the God of Elijah who sent it (1 Kings 18:20-46).

Although Elijah's ministry had been effective in discrediting Baal and in reducing the number of Baal-worshippers, the cult still posed a threat to Israel. Error dies hard. It is not surprising, therefore, that the Lord should bring Elijah's ministry to an end in such a way as to demonstrate once again the fraudulence of Baal. By causing Elijah to ride on the clouds, the Lord did this. He showed that it was he, and not Baal, who controls the heavens.

The triumph of God's Word

Throughout his ministry Elijah was, in effect, the very embodiment of the Word of God. By sweeping the prophet up into heaven the Lord was honouring his Word and at the same time declaring its final triumph.

This must have come as a tremendous consolation to Elisha. He was about to step into the role that Elijah had occupied by serving as the primary bearer of the Word of God in Israel. The times were very difficult and discouraging, and Elisha would almost certainly have moments when it would seem as if the cause of God was all but lost. But the cause of God would not fail. The Word of God which Elisha was called to proclaim would finally win out over all false gods and false teachings.

An anticipation of Christ's ascension

It is impossible to read about Elijah's translation into heaven without our thoughts gravitating towards the ascension of the Lord Jesus Christ (Luke 24:50-51; Acts 1:9).

Elijah's translation indicated that God was pleased with his faithful ministry. Although he was faithful to God, Elijah was still a flawed man. He was, James writes, 'a man with a nature like ours' (James 5:17). No one has ever been perfectly faithful except the Lord Jesus Christ. His faithful ministry was not tarnished by any sin (1 John 3:5). He spoke perfectly the words the Father gave him to speak. He performed perfectly the works the Father had sent him to perform. He did not deviate from the path of obedience that was set before him.

The supreme climax of his obedience was his death on the cross. He died as no one has done before or since. That death was designed by God as the means for redeeming guilty sinners. It was a substitutionary death. Jesus had no sins of his own for which he had to endure the wrath of God, but in his death on the cross he bore that wrath in the place of his people. When he cried from the cross, 'It is finished!' (John 19:30), he signalled his completion of the task assigned to him by the Father.

The Father responded to this perfect work by raising Christ from the grave and receiving him into heaven. This constituted the Father's approval of a perfect mission carried out with perfect faithfulness.

Our Lord's performance of his task was so complete that his ascension, unlike Elijah's translation, did not include a transition to a successor. Nothing in redemption's plan was left for another to complete. Christ alone is the Redeemer and Saviour.

The epilogue: Elisha is confirmed as Elijah's successor (2:13-18)

Elijah had promised that Elisha would receive his request if he saw Elijah taken up (2:10). Elisha had indeed seen the spectacular sight (2:12). He had also seen Elijah's mantle drop to the ground, and he now picked it up as a tangible sign and token that his request had been granted. He was now Elijah's successor.

It was important that other prophets should realize that there was no reason to despair about the cause of the Lord. Elijah's work would be carried on by Elisha. To confirm Elisha's position in the eyes of the other prophets, the Lord immediately used him to do two things.

His miraculous crossing of the Jordan (2:13-15)

With Elijah's mantle in his hand, Elisha went back to the Jordan river, struck the water with the mantle and cried, **'Where is the Lord God of Elijah?'** (2:14). With this cry Elisha was essentially calling upon God to help him. The mantle was the symbol of God's promise to grant him the spirit and power of Elijah. Elisha was now asking God to manifest that spirit and demonstrate that power. He was asking God to confirm for him the promise that he had been given when Elijah's mantle fell to the ground.

We can well understand Elisha crying out for help. He was to stand for God in the face of rampant apostasy. He could not hope to succeed apart from the Lord God showing himself strong on his behalf.

Elisha's cry for help represents a profound and striking contrast with the behaviour of the people of Judah during the time of the prophet Jeremiah. The men and women of that day, along with the priests, would be in desperate need of the help of God, but they would refuse to take up the cry of Elisha. Jeremiah says:

Neither did they say, 'Where is the Lord,
Who brought us up out of the land of Egypt...?' ...

The priests did not say, 'Where is the LORD?'
And those who handle the law did not know me...
                                        (Jer. 2:6,8).

Elisha's cry for help was answered as the water of the Jordan immediately parted and allowed the prophet to cross over in exactly the same way that he and Elijah had done (2:8). There could now be no doubt among the prophets that the spirit of Elijah was resting on Elisha (2:15). The *New Geneva Study Bible* observes: 'God designated Joshua as the approved successor to Moses ... by having Joshua lead the people across the Jordan River into the Promised Land, much as Moses led the people through the Red Sea... Now God designates Elisha as the successor to Elijah by dividing the Jordan for him as He did for Elijah...'[2]

We cannot help but think that Elijah deliberately orchestrated his final journey in such a way to draw a contrast between the people of Israel at this time and when they entered the land of Canaan. On that earlier occasion they had crossed over the Jordan river, and then gone in succession to Jericho, Gilgal and Bethel. Here Elijah and Elisha reverse the order, going from Bethel, Gilgal and Jericho before crossing over the Jordan. When the people of Israel entered Canaan, they were, of course, on their way out of captivity in Egypt. It could very well be that Elijah intended his final journey to declare the solemn truth that the nation was on its way back into captivity. Such symbolism would not have been lost on Elisha, who may have intended his return crossing of the Jordan to declare that Israel would experience yet another exodus.

The fruitless search for Elijah's body (2:16-18)

Elisha's role as Elijah's successor was also confirmed to the prophets when he accurately predicted that they would not find Elijah's body. The prophets had put pressure on Elisha to permit this search. They may very well have thought that only Elijah's soul was taken into heaven. Or they may have thought that Elijah was only taken part of the way up before being cast down to earth. Elisha finally consented to the search which, as he had said, proved to be futile. The prophets now knew that Elisha had seen something of an incredibly astonishing nature and this gave him even more stature in their eyes.

What this has to say to us

This chapter speaks very forcefully to us. God not only demonstrated in Elijah's translation that his cause was not going to fail, but also that he had a plan to preserve that cause on the earth at that time. What was his plan? It involved a man named Elisha. He had used Elijah as his instrument and he was now about to use Elisha.

3.
Elisha goes to work

Please read 2 Kings 2:19-25

With this passage we come to the ministry of the prophet Elisha. While Elisha succeeded Elijah, he conducted a ministry that was very different from that of his predecessor. While Elijah's ministry featured the wrath and judgement of God, that of Elisha demonstrated the mercy and compassion of God. This should not be construed to mean that Elisha's ministry was in some way superior. Both men were called by God to be prophets and both fulfilled the Lord's purpose.

Elisha's ministry also featured an explosion of miracles, sixteen in all. Lorraine Boettner defines a miracle in this way: '... an event in the external world, wrought by the immediate power of God, and designed to accredit a message or messenger'.[1] A miracle is an appearance of the supernatural within the realm of the natural with the intent of furthering God's purposes.

Two extremes on miracles

The element of the miraculous in the Bible inevitably leads to one of two extremes among professing Christians. On the one hand, some deny that most of the miracles of the Bible ever took place. As far as they are concerned, God has left the world to operate completely on the basis of natural laws. This view attacks the very heart and soul of Christianity. It denies the testimony of Scripture and the Bible's message of redemption. If there is no possibility of miracles, Jesus was not God in human flesh and did not arise from the grave, and if these are not true, there is no eternal salvation.

The other extreme is to suggest that miracles should be the constant and ongoing experience of all Christians. (Just how the miraculous can be commonplace and still be miraculous is something of a puzzle!) Those who hold this position fail to recognize that the miracles of the Bible are not spread evenly throughout. They are contained in four clusters:

1. Under Moses when the Lord was delivering Israel from Egypt and establishing her as a nation;
2. During the ministries of Elijah and Elisha;
3. During the Babylonian captivity of the Jews;
4. During the ministry of the Lord Jesus Christ and shortly after his ascension.

It should be noted that each of these clusters occurred at a time of great crisis or transition, always for the good of God's people as a whole and with a view to furthering God's plan of redemption. Many of the so-called miracles today seem to be more in the nature of a private luxury, with a view to making life more easy and comfortable for certain individuals.

We should not be surprised to find an abundance of miracles during the ministries of Elijah and Elisha. Theirs was a critical time in the life of Israel, a time in which the nation had lurched headlong into the worship of Baal. God sent Elijah and Elisha to arrest the downward course of Israel and draw her back to the Lord, and the Lord attested their ministries by doing many miracles.

Two miracles

In the verses before us, we find two miracles. In the first Elisha purified some contaminated water (2:19-22). In the second he pronounced a curse on a group of rebellious youths (2:23-24). These two miracles are tied together by the common thread of a curse. In the first a curse is removed and in the second a curse is put in place.

A curse removed (2:19-22)

The city of Jericho, after lying desolate from the time of Joshua (Josh. 6:24,26), had finally been rebuilt by Hiel of Bethel (1 Kings 16:34). Hiel paid a dreadful price for his building project, burying his two sons in the process and fulfilling the prophecy of Joshua (Josh. 6:26). Although the city was now inhabited, remnants of God's curse upon it remained. The water supply was so contaminated that it even made the land barren (2:19).

The men of the city appealed to the prophet for help, and Elisha responded by asking them to put salt into a new bowl. He then went to the source of the water, cast in the salt and said, **'Thus says the LORD: "I have healed this water; from it there shall be no more death or barrenness"'** (2:21).

This cure at one and the same time authenticated Elisha as God's prophet and illustrated the nature of true salvation. It did the latter in that salt is a cleanser and preservative. C. F. Keil observes: 'Salt, according to its power of preserving from corruption and decomposition, is a symbol of incorruptibility and of the power of life which destroys death.'[2]

Pouring salt from a bowl to purify contaminated water! Elisha's cure must have seemed utterly ridiculous and totally out of keeping with the seriousness of the situation, but it proved to be effective. The water was immediately and permanently purified (2:22).

A curse pronounced (2:23-25)

The second miracle in these verses occurred when Elisha went to Bethel. There he encountered some rebellious youths who mocked him.

The Authorized / King James Version calls these **'little children'**, but they were probably young men. We must not think of these young men as nice, polite fellows who happened upon Elisha as they were returning from Sunday School and decided to enjoy an innocent joke at his expense. These were young thugs. We would probably not miss the mark by much if we thought of them as the ancient equivalent of the gangs that roam the streets of our major cities.

We should give due weight to the fact that these young toughs were from Bethel, a centre of idolatrous worship since Jeroboam had established the northern kingdom of Israel (1 Kings 12:25-33). If there was any place in Israel where a prophet of the Lord would not be welcome, it was Bethel. It is probable that these youths had drunk deeply from the hostility of Bethel towards the things of God. They saw in Elisha the opportunity to vent some of that hostility. They raced towards the prophet, circled him and began screaming: **'Go up, you baldhead! Go up, you baldhead!'** (2:23). Having heard accounts of Elijah's being translated, these young rebels were calling upon the bald-headed Elisha to do the same. It may very well have been their way of telling him that they did not want a prophet of the Lord anywhere near them. As far as they were concerned, the world was not large enough for themselves and a prophet of the Lord.

Some have suggested that these young men may have desired to see the prophet translated because of a lust for the sensational. The Lord Jesus had to deal with people who followed him in the hope of seeing him do a miracle rather than out of interest in the truth. When some scribes and Pharisees asked him to perform a sign, Jesus said, 'An evil and adulterous generation seeks after a sign...' (Matt. 12:39).

Whatever the motivation of the young men who taunted Elisha, the prophet was not amused. The author says, **'So he turned around and looked at them, and pronounced a curse on them in the name of the LORD'** (2:24). The author then describes what happened: **'And two female bears came out of the woods and mauled forty-two of the youths'** (2:24). The text does not explicitly say that Elisha called for two bears to come out of the woods and attack the young men, but rather that he 'pronounced a curse on them in the name of the LORD'. It was the Lord who sent the bears to maul these young men. We should also note that while many commentators assume that all of these youths were killed, the account does not specifically say so. Some may very well have been killed, but most of them probably escaped with severe wounds. This was an example of God's wrath upon those who hate him.

Pictures of gospel realities

As God's prophet, Elisha was cast into the role of a mediator between God and the people. Because of this role Elisha should always be viewed as a type of the Lord Jesus Christ, and we must look at the prophet's actions for pictures of the gospel of Christ.

With this in mind we look for gospel truths in the miracles of Jericho and Bethel. These miracles, so far removed from our own time, speak to us very powerfully about realities that are just as true today as they were then.

God's purification of the polluted

The miracle of the purified waters may be regarded as a picture of the very heart of the gospel message. The truth is that we are by nature every bit as polluted and contaminated as the waters of Jericho. We come into this world with the very well-spring of life itself polluted by sin, and that pollution guarantees a spiritual barrenness in our lives in the same way that the polluted waters of Jericho ensured barrenness for the land. The apostle Paul asserts that pollution when he tells believers in Ephesians that they were 'by nature children of wrath' (Eph. 2:3).

Our natural pollution with sin does not mean that we are as bad as we can possibly be. It rather means that no part of our lives is free from the taint or influence of sin. Our minds are darkened by sin so we cannot understand the truth of God (1 Cor. 2:14: 2 Cor. 4:4). Our affections are so degraded by sin that we do not naturally love God, but are rather at enmity with him (Rom. 8:7). Our wills are so deadened by sin that we do not desire God or choose him (Rom. 3:11).

There are yet more parallels. As God provided a way for the contaminated water of Jericho to be purified, so he has provided a way for us to be purified. That way looks to many to be as ludicrous as the new bowl and the salt used by Elisha. The way by which God reverses our soul-pollution is the death of his own Son, Jesus Christ, on a Roman cross. The world is quick to suggest that this death could not possibly have anything to do with putting away sin, but it is through that unlikely instrument that God cleanses his people of their pollution. That apparently absurd death saves! It is the very wisdom and power of God to that end (1 Cor. 1:18-25).

God's judgement on the mockers

God's action in the death of his Son does not mean that the curse of sin is automatically removed for all. Those who mock God's truth and reject his salvation will eventually experience God's judgement. There is no shortage of evidence for this. The people of Israel mocked their prophets 'until the wrath of the LORD arose against his people, till there was no remedy' (2 Chr. 36:16).

And we remember that while Jesus was on the cross he was tormented with mockery that was the opposite of that directed to Elisha. While the prophet was told to 'Go up', the Lord was asked to 'Come down' (Matt. 27:29,31,41-44). The rejection of Christ, so wickedly expressed in that mockery, resulted in the destruction of Jerusalem by the Romans in A.D. 70, just as Jesus himself had predicted (Luke 19:41-44).

No story in the Old Testament has aroused a greater out-pouring of criticism than God's judgement on those who mocked Elisha. Many suggest that it constitutes a misrepresentation of God. They tell us we must not look here to find out what God is like but must rather look to the Lord Jesus Christ.

But what do we see when we look to Christ? For one thing, we find the Lord Jesus speaking very forcefully about the reality of eternal judgement (Matt. 25:31-46; Mark 9:42-50; Luke 16:19-31). And when we look at the cross of Jesus Christ, we find not only, as some suggest, the love of God, but also such wrath that the Lord Jesus Christ, who bore it in the stead of his people, cried out, 'My God, my God, why have you forsaken me?' (Matt. 27:46). The love of Calvary is great for precisely this reason: Jesus Christ endured the wrath of God so that his people will never have to endure it (2 Cor. 5:21; 1 Peter 3:18).

Although Ananias and Sapphira lived after Christ's first coming, they could give eloquent testimony to the ongoing reality of God's wrath (Acts 5:1-11).

We would do well, then, to heed the curse that fell at Bethel lest God's wrath fall upon us. The temporal judgement that befell these young men was designed to be a warning to every generation of the eternal judgement that awaits all who respond to the truths of God with contempt.

As we contemplate the two miracles that began Elisha's ministry, we cannot help but note that Jericho went from a curse (Josh 6:26) to a blessing, while Bethel went from a blessing (Gen. 28:10-22) to a curse. All who are living spiritually at Bethel (the place of curse) would do well to move to Jericho (the place of blessing) without delay.

> Kiss the Son, lest he be angry,
> And you perish in the way,
> When his wrath is kindled but a little.
> Blessed are those who put their trust in him
>
> (Ps. 2:12).

A message for the church

We should not leave the miracles at Jericho and Bethel without thinking of how they would have spoken to the captives in Babylon. The exiles would undoubtedly have read this account with a view to their own situation and how they came to be in it. They had attributed to Baal the authority that belonged to God alone and, when they were confronted by the messengers God sent, had mocked them. Elisha's deeds at Jericho and Bethel would have made them realize what fools they had been. The miracle at Jericho gave additional testimony to their folly in going after Baal because it showed that God alone had power over the waters. The miracle at Bethel showed their folly in mocking the prophets. They, like the young men, had been guilty of mockery and they, like those who poured scorn on Elisha, had come under judgement.

It is the same today. Those who mock God's truth (and to mock his messengers is to mock God) and turn to idols invite God's displeasure.

4.
Help for the helpless

Please read 2 Kings 3:1-27

This chapter details the military expedition of three kings against a fourth, Mesha, the King of Moab. It was the latter's decision to cease paying tribute to Israel that led to this campaign being mounted.

The expedition was led by Jehoram, King of Israel. He, another son of Ahab, was, like his father, a graceless man. The author of 2 Kings gives him credit for removing the **'sacred pillar of Baal that his father had made'** (3:2), which probably consisted of a relief of Baal and an inscription. We should not be overly impressed with this one act. Jehoram was a devotee of the false religion of Bethel which was initiated by Jeroboam when the kingdom of Solomon split (3:3; see 1 Kings 12:25-33).

This expedition also included Jehoshaphat, King of Judah. Although he was a very godly man, he was all too prone to associate himself with the vile and wicked kings of Israel. He had done this when Ahab was on the throne of Israel, and had almost lost his life in the process (1 Kings 22:1-8,29-32; 2 Chr. 18:1-3; 19:1-3). In this chapter, he again manifests this alarming tendency and, in doing so, serves as a reminder to God's people in every generation to avoid evil company. The apostle Paul says, 'Evil company corrupts good habits' (1 Cor. 15:33).

Finally, this expedition also included the King of Edom. As one of Israel's vassals, he, like the high priest's servant in the New Testament (Luke 22:50), would have had little choice about being included.

Three helpless kings

The three kings of this expedition were bound together in another way — that is, in their helplessness to deal with the situation in which they found themselves. Their plan to take a long, roundabout route in their march against Moab, by way of the Wilderness of Edom, caused their supply of water to be depleted (3:8-9). They were now an army in the wilderness without water. The kings had everyone at their beck and call. They could command their servants to run here and there to do this and that, but they could not produce water. They were helpless in the face of this crisis. Joseph Hall writes, 'What are the greatest monarchs of the world, if they want but water to their mouths?'[1]

It is interesting to notice the different responses to this crisis. Jehoram, who had no place for God, said of this dilemma, **'Alas! For the LORD has called these three kings together to deliver them into the hand of Moab'** (3:10). Even though he openly denied God, Jehoram could not erase from his conscience the knowledge that God was real and that he, Jehoram, stood guilty before the Lord and deserved only his wrath. The reality of God is writ so large in the human conscience that sinners deliberately suppress it. We might say they put the truth of God in a box, nail it shut and sit on the lid, but even having done all that, they cannot entirely rid themselves of it.

Godly Jehoshaphat responded to the crisis in this way: **'Is there no prophet of the LORD here, that we may enquire of the LORD by him?'** (3:11). Although he was where he did not belong, Jehoshaphat did not forget God. Faced with the crisis, he went to the Lord. Walter Brueggemann observes: 'Jehoshaphat ... understands that there is a "surplus dimension" to historical reality. And that surplus which goes beyond royal strategies concerns the will of the Lord, which cannot be ignored.'[2]

Jehoshaphat realized that the situation was such that only the true God could help. Brueggemann well says, 'It does not take long for history to press the human managers beyond their resources. Life has a terror and an inscrutability that requires another word, another discernment, another act based on different resources.'[3]

When faced with such a crisis, God's people know what to do. They know where to find that other word and other discernment that the crisis demands. They know to go to God and his Word.

One of the immense tragedies of this day is that so many who profess to be among God's people seem to be bent on marginalizing God and his Word. Instead of offering 'another word, another discernment,' to those who are up against life's crises, they are content to look to the latest psychological 'insights'. The bankruptcy of those who have bartered God's Word away for the latest trend is never more apparent than when they try to help those who are face to face with life's greatest crisis — that is, going out into eternity.

A sufficient God

It is at this point that the grace of God begins to shine in this passage. There is wickedness everywhere — Jehoram was a wicked man, the godly Jehoshaphat was consorting with him and the two were engaged in a venture that had not been sanctioned by the Lord — but in the midst of it all God was still gracious.

The grace of God's revelation

While many commentators seem to assume that Elisha had joined in this doubtful venture from the beginning, Scripture does not say as much. It could very well be that he came on the scene shortly before he was needed for the express purpose of delivering the Word of God to the kings.

God could have withheld his Word in this situation, but he graciously granted it through Elisha. The prophet began by roundly rebuking Jehoram: **'What have I to do with you? Go to the prophets of your father and the prophets of your mother'** (3:13).

Elisha went on to state that he would not have had anything at all to do with this situation were it not for the godly Jehoshaphat (3:14). In other words, there would have been no blessing at all for Israel or Edom were it not for God's covenant with the house of David. God always blesses sinners not because of any merits of their own, but rather because of his covenant with his Son.

After calling for music (3:15), probably to soothe him after his spirit was agitated by the presence of Jehoram, Elisha delivered God's Word for the occasion — namely, that the combined armies of Israel, Judah and Edom were to dig ditches in the valley (3:16) and those ditches would be miraculously filled with water without the armies detecting any wind or seeing any rain (3:17). The Lord would also use those ditches to bring defeat to Moab (3:18). F. W. Krummacher says of Elisha on this occasion: 'How cheering is this voice crying in such a dreary wilderness!'[4]

The Word of God continues to sound in dreary wildernesses. To those who are in the wilderness of sin and unbelief, the Word of God offers forgiveness from God and eternal life. To those Christians who are in the wilderness of discouragement, the Word of God promises that he will never leave us nor forsake us. God has a word for every situation in which we find ourselves.

The grace of God's deliverance

There is a twofold deliverance in this chapter. The first is deliverance from the lack of water. The second is the deliverance of Moab into the hands of the three kings.

Deliverance from lack of water

First, God delivered the armies of Israel, Judah and Edom from their lack of water. God did this by filling the ditches with water. How did he do this? Did he merely create the water? Such a thing would have been no problem for the one who created all the oceans in the beginning! Did he cause the water to rise up from underground caverns? Or did he send rain in the distant mountains and cause the water to run down to fill these ditches in the valley? It is not important how God accomplished this. What is important is that he did exactly as he had promised.

Deliverance of Moab to the three kings

God performed this second deliverance by causing the soldiers of Moab to be deluded. When they saw the reddish cast of the ditches full of water, created by the sun shining on the water (3:22), they concluded that they were seeing blood. Assuming that the armies of Israel, Judah and Edom had turned upon each other and that nothing now remained except to collect the spoils, they rushed headlong into destruction (3:22-24). The message of Elisha the prophet was confirmed to the last detail.

God's delivering grace is not restricted to these ancient episodes. It is a present and ongoing reality. God repeats the miracle of supplying water each time he grants salvation to a sinner. The sinner can be likened to a dry and parched land, and the gospel to refreshing water. The Lord Jesus made this connection on more than one occasion (John 4:10-14; 7:37-39).

We may also take God's deliverance of Moab into the hands of Israel and Judah as a tiny picture of that glorious day in which he will put down all the enemies of his people for ever (1 Cor. 15:20-28). Because of this all God's people heartily consent to David's words:

> You prepare a table before me in the presence of my
> enemies;
> You anoint my head with oil;
> My cup runs over.
> Surely goodness and mercy shall follow me
> All the days of my life;
> And I will dwell in the house of the LORD
> For ever
>
> (Ps. 23:5-6).

A fourth helpless king

The closing verses of this chapter have generated considerable debate among commentators. These verses tell us that Mesha, the King of Moab, sacrificed his eldest son, the crown prince of the nation (3:27). This sacrifice was presumably made to Chemosh, the god of the Moabites, in the hope that he would stop the marauding army of Israel. This sacrifice culminated in **'great indignation against Israel'** (3:27).

Some think God felt this indignation against Israel because her army went far beyond what was necessary in subduing

Moab and in so doing drove the King of Moab to desperation. Others think Judah and Edom felt the indignation against Israel for the same reason — that is, that Israel was pressing the military effort too strongly. Others think Moab felt the indignation against Israel also for that reason.

There is a problem with suggesting that the Israelites went too far. Elisha, the prophet of the Lord, commanded them to do what they did (3:19). As God's prophet, he spoke for God. It is more likely that the army of Israel, sickened by the sight of human sacrifice, lifted the siege. John Gill concludes: '... the three kings ... when they saw the Moabites would sell their lives so dear, and hold out to the last man, they thought fit to break up the siege; and perhaps were greatly affected with the barbarous shocking sight they had seen, and might fear, should they stay, something else of the like kind would be done.'[5]

One thing that does lie right on the surface, however, is the helpless condition of those who are not visited by the grace of God. There is, as we have noticed, plenty of wickedness in this chapter. But there is also a great difference between the wicked act of Jehoshaphat, who had been visited by the grace of God, and the desperate wickedness of a Mesha, who did not know this grace. While not condoning Jehoshaphat's sin of consorting with the wicked, God continued to manifest his grace to him. Mesha, on the other hand, was left completely to himself.

If we, like Jehoshaphat, have been visited by the grace of God, we should rejoice exceedingly and serve the Lord faithfully. What a timely reminder this was for the first readers of 2 Kings, the captives in Babylon! They were in captivity because they had failed to prize as they should the grace of God that had worked in their nation, and their future success depended on their having an entirely different attitude towards that grace. What a cheering thought it must have been for these people to realize that their situation was not hopeless! The God who could make water in the ditches could and would help them.

On the other hand, those who, like Mesha, have not been visited by that grace should seek it, knowing as they do that such seeking is already an indication that God has granted it.

5.
An abounding supply
for surpassing demands

Please read 2 Kings 4:1-7

The widow in this passage is only identified as **'a certain woman of the wives of the sons of the prophets'** (4:1). However, her value to us resides not in how much space she occupies in Scripture, or in the amount of information we have about her, but rather in the single great lesson she has to teach us. Here is a woman who demonstrates for all generations the way to face surpassing demands when we find ourselves with only meagre resources. She shows us that the abounding resources of the Word of God become ours to the degree that we place our faith in them.

This lesson will become quite clear and obvious as we consider the surpassing demands this woman faced, her meagre resources and her wise strategy.

The surpassing demands she faced

This passage wastes no time in introducing us to the surpassing demands this woman was facing. Her husband had died, and she was left with two sons and a substantial debt. Her creditor, a human iceberg, had decided that her sons would make a highly suitable payment for her debt, and he was soon to come and take them as his slaves.

This woman was mystified by it all. The perplexity she felt is evident in her plaintive cry to Elisha: **'Your servant my husband is dead, and you know that your servant feared the LORD'** (4:1). Her husband had faithfully served the Lord and had died young. She had fully shared his commitment to the Lord and she was now left with a huge debt and the impending slavery of her sons. We would like to believe that serving God makes us exempt from the troubles of life, that God spares us such things because of our service; but it is not so. We want this passage to say this woman and her husband served the Lord and they lived happily ever after; but it does not.

Some would have us believe that there was a serious flaw in the faith and service of this woman and her husband. They insist that there is no need for the children of God ever to be ill or to experience financial reversals. If they do, then, these people claim, it is because they have failed in faith. But this passage finds no fault with the faith and service of this woman or of her husband, and yet she not only suffers, but does so in the most heart-rending manner imaginable.

Her meagre resources

The author of this passage moves immediately from the crushing demands that faced this woman to highlight her meagre resources. She was confronted with overwhelming, enormous debt, and all she had left to her name was one rather pathetic jar of oil. Hear her sad testimony to the prophet: **'Your maidservant has nothing in the house but a jar of oil'** (4:2).

It is bad enough to find ourselves a few dollars short of the total when we face a debt, but this woman wasn't anywhere near being able to pay. A huge debt was coupled with the slenderest of resources! I have often heard people lament their financial situation by saying, 'We have even had to dip into our savings.' But this woman had no savings into which she could 'dip'. She had no collateral, stocks or bonds. All she had was her little jar of oil.

Picture it. The creditor arrives at her door and demands payment, and she hands over the pathetic little jar and asks, 'Would you accept this as payment?' The creditor, after laughing, would most certainly have said, 'Do you take me for a fool?' And then he would have made off with her two sons. Her jar of oil did not begin to approach the magnitude of the debt, any more than a penny would come anywhere near settling a debt of a thousand pounds.

Most of us have no difficulty at all identifying with this sad combination of surpassing demands and meagre resources. We all too often find ourselves feeling as if we are caught in precisely the same situation.

The surpassing demands we face may not relate to money matters. The financial situation of the widow in this story may legitimately be taken to represent crushing demands of every kind. Perhaps in our case the crushing demand is the serious illness that stalks life itself, and we seem to have nothing more than a little jar of strength and comfort in the midst of it all. Perhaps the demand on us has to do with responsibilities that are numerous and great, and we seem to have just a little jar of strength and wisdom for facing them. The demand may be a wretched home situation. It may be a marriage that is ready to fall apart, or children that seem to be set on breaking our hearts. We find ourselves desperately yearning for guidance and grace, but, alas, all we have is our little jar.

The truth is that we all desperately need this episode of the widow and her huge debt and meagre resources. We need it, not merely to identify with her problems, but rather so than we can adopt a similar approach in dealing with the demands that we face.

Her wise strategy

What did this woman do about her situation? She went to the man of God, Elisha, and there she found a sufficient resource for her searing trial.

Elisha told her what to do. She was to borrow empty vessels from her neighbours — not just a few, but many (4:3). And then she and her sons were to take that little jar of oil and begin to pour oil into those empty vessels (4:4).

The woman did as Elisha commanded. She and her sons borrowed as many vessels as they could. Then they began to pour oil from their little jar. The first empty vessel was filled, then the next, and the next, until all were brimming full — and it was all from that one little jar of oil (4:5-6).

The woman and her sons now had more than enough oil to sell and pay off their debt (4:7). The surpassing demand which they faced had been met by a sufficient resource.

What can we learn from this incident?

This account would have been very meaningful to the captives in Babylon. They did not have the resources for the demands that their experience placed upon them. But God had sent his Word with them into Babylon, and that Word was sufficient to sustain them there.

The sons of the prophets would also have found this account to be most helpful. The prophets were called to minister in exceedingly difficult times. They often felt themselves taxed to the limit, but the Word of God that they proclaimed was sufficient for them.

What about us? What does this story say to us? Here we are facing all kinds of demands of our own, demands for which we so often have very little strength. What is our little jar of oil? Where can we find a sufficiency for the demands we face?

The key for us is to focus, not so much on the little jar of oil, but on Elisha the prophet. It was his word that made the jar of oil effective and sufficient. Perhaps we find ourselves wishing that we could have a prophet like Elisha, one to whom we could go in the crises of life and find help and guidance. Thank God, we do have our Elisha. No, we do not have a flesh-and-blood prophet such as he, but we do have the Word of God. Let us always remember that God's prophets were men in whom the Word of God resided. It was that Word which made them what they were.

Now God's word on this occasion was for this woman to gather the vessels and pour oil into them from her one jar. Have you ever considered how ridiculous and demanding the Word of God was for this woman? It required her to go from one neighbour to the next to borrow vessels. And, of course, each neighbour had to have an explanation: 'Why are you collecting empty jars?' And the widow was compelled to say time after time, 'I am going to fill them all from my one little jar of oil.' How would you like to go around the neighbourhood collecting empty containers and offering that explanation? But the Word of God proved to be true for the widow and her sons!

That same Word of God offers help to each and every one of us for the demands we face. It is a veritable gold mine of comfort and assurance. It brims with promises. It overflows with examples of those who have trusted God. It gleams with precepts and commands to guide us.

If you are sick, it points you to one who cares for you and sticks closer to you than a brother. If you are confused about which way to turn, it tells you not to lean on your own understanding but rather to trust the Lord (Prov. 3:5-6). If you are dying, it tells you of a heavenly home into which the Lord will receive all those who know him. If your home is falling apart, that same Word tells you not to insist on your own way, but to submit to the teachings of your God and the example of your Christ. No matter what your trial, you can and must pour the soothing oil of God's Word into the empty vessel of your life. Yes, pour and keep pouring!

We must remember that the abounding resources of the Word of God become ours to the degree that we place our faith in that Word. God's Word abounded in the life of the widow because she placed great faith in it. She was not content to gather only a vessel or two. She gathered many, and she received an abounding supply. Many want the Word of God to abound with comfort, strength and help, but they do not want to abound in their faith in that Word and in the practice of its precepts. God's Word is so often with us the way it was with this woman. It often seems ridiculous and very demanding, and we can easily find ourselves reluctant to admit in this sophisticated age that we believe this Word, but believe it we must if we want to receive sufficient strength for our trials.

The primary application of this passage is to Christians finding in the Word of God the sufficient resource they need for facing the surpassing demands of life. But there is an application for unbelievers who are, even if they do not realize it, facing a demand that surpasses all others. When they leave this life, they must stand before the God who is the Judge of all the earth. Unlike the widow in this story, they have, not a meagre resource, but no resource at all for this meeting.

All would seem to be hopeless, but the Word of God holds out a sufficient resource. It is none other than the Lord Jesus Christ himself and his redeeming death on Calvary's cross. The Bible tells us that the only way we can ever stand in the presence of God is on the basis of Christ's death, that we must repent of our sins and cast ourselves entirely upon him. It seems to be an utterly ridiculous message, as ridiculous as Elisha telling this woman to gather empty vessels and fill them from one vessel. But it is God's message, and if you are to receive the salvation Christ has made available, you must believe that message. If you do, you will find in Christ a sufficient resource for the coming Day of Judgement.

Christians are those who, like the widow, have had their debts paid by God. Raymond Dillard poignantly observes: 'The greatest debt we all have is the mortgage on our souls. It is a debt we cannot pay. But God can pay it. He has paid it by giving his own Son as a ransom for our souls.'[1]

6.
Wonderful displays of God's mercy and power

Please read 2 Kings 4:8-37

This passage brings together two remarkable people of faith — the Shunammite woman and the prophet Elisha. But neither is the hero of the story presented here. God is the hero, as he is of every story of the Bible.

In this particular episode the Bible casts its spotlight on the mercy and power of God. To appreciate this fully we must remind ourselves that this episode occurred during a terrible time of apostasy in the nation of Israel. The worship of Baal was still present and the false religion established by Jeroboam was continuing to thrive and flourish. But in the midst of it all, God displayed his mercy and power.

Terence E. Fretheim notes: 'Apostasy and its effects have not taken over God's world. Needs are being met; life is being given and restored; God the Creator is still at work for good... God's good creation is *properly* at work in the midst of those who would disrupt it'[1] (italics are his).

What encouragement this provides for us! We too live in a time of apostasy and idolatry, but the wickedness of men cannot dethrone God. He still works in the midst of it all.

The birth of a son (4:8-17)

God first expressed his mercy and power to the Shunammite woman and her husband by giving them a son.

Because the Shunammite had shown great kindness to Elisha by providing a place for him to stop on his travels (4:8-10), the prophet desired to do something to show his gratitude. After the woman herself refused his suggestions on how he might help her (4:13), his servant Gehazi called his attention to the fact that she was childless. Furthermore, her husband's advanced age seemed to preclude any possibility of her having a child. Although the woman had not complained about being childless or asked for a child, Elisha promised she would embrace a son in about a year. Elisha's prediction seemed too good to be true, but it was fulfilled (4:16-17).

Of course, Elisha was not the source of this miracle, but merely its instrument. Only God could override such a hopeless situation and cause this son to be born. In so doing, he repeated the miracle he had performed for Abraham and Sarah (Gen. 21:1-3), Isaac and Rebekah (Gen. 25:21), Jacob and Rachel (Gen. 30:22-23) and Elkanah and Hannah (1 Sam. 1:8-20). The same miracle would occur again in the case of Zacharias and Elizabeth (Luke 1:5-25).

The death of the son (4:18-20)

Some years later, the story takes an unexpected and devastating turn. The child is suddenly stricken with severe pain in his head and dies (4:18-20). This calamity reminds us of the same truth we noticed with the widow woman and her two sons (4:1-7) — namely, that even the most godly suffer hardship and difficulty.

The death of her son was such a severe trial that the Shunammite might have been tempted to give up her faith. She could have said something like this: 'What's the use? I have lived for the Lord and this is what I get in return.' What faith this woman demonstrated! She refused to accept death as the final word. She placed the body of her son in the room she had prepared for Elisha and set out for Mt Carmel to find the prophet himself (4:25). She clung to Elisha even as Gehazi tried to push her away (4:27). She then poured out her plight to the prophet with these words: **'Did I ask a son of my lord? Did I not say, "Do not deceive me"?'** (4:28).

This woman gives us insight into the true nature of faith. It is not mere positive thinking. It is not a matter of someone selecting something that he wants to be true and persuading himself that it will be true. Faith is believing what God himself has revealed. It is resting on his Word. The fact that God had specifically given this child as a comfort to the woman and her husband indicated that he did not intend that the child's death should be final. God's miraculous provision of the child was in and of itself a promise that the child was to live.

Furthermore, the Shunammite had probably been told by Elisha himself the story of Elijah at the widow's house in Zarephath (1 Kings 17:17-24). There also God took the woman's son after seemingly indicating that both he and his mother would survive the drought. Death did not have the final word on that occasion as God used Elijah to raise the boy from the dead.

Fortified by these things, the Shunammite refused to give up. Her words to her husband and to the messenger of the prophet that all was well (4:23,26) clearly show that she was clinging in faith to God.

Raymond B. Dillard writes, 'Faith is continuing to believe in the promises and goodness of God. Faith is considering it certain that God will be true to his word. It is knowing that he is able to do immeasurably more than all we ask or imagine (Eph. 3:20). God does not mislead or deceive us (2 Kings 4:16,28).'² But why would the child die if God did not intend his death to be final? We are here in the dark recesses of God's providential dealings with his people. We cannot begin to decipher such things. We do know, however, that God sends difficulties into the lives of his children for wonderful purposes. Through such events he weans us away from the things of the world and casts us more entirely upon himself. By such means he reveals more of himself and his ways to us and leads us into closer communion and intimacy with himself.

The Shunammite was not alone in this faith. Elisha joined her in believing that the death of the child was a temporary test designed to open the door to a far greater expression of God's mercy and power in her life.

The resurrection of the son (4:29-37)

As soon as he realized the Shunammite's child was dead, Elisha gave his staff to Gehazi and sent him ahead to lay it on the face of the child (4:29-30). Gehazi did as instructed without results (4:31). Gehazi had Elisha's rod but not the faith with which to use it. He reminds us that merely going through the form of religion is not enough and that a ministry conducted apart from the presence of the living God is useless.

Elisha and the woman arrived later and prayed for the child, but again there was no result (4:33).

Elisha then stretched himself upon the child as Elijah had done when he raised the son of the widow of Zarephath (1 Kings 17:21-22). This strategy was effective as the child sneezed seven times and opened his eyes (4:35). Imagine the gratitude and sheer, unfettered joy of the Shunammite as she wrapped her living son in her arms.

This resurrection abundantly demonstrated God's mercy and power, mercy in that God was willing to raise this child and power in that he was able to do it.

God's mercy and power did not come to an end that day. He has not exhausted these qualities but still manifests them in the lives of his children. Every child of God is a testimony to that same mercy and power because every child of God has already experienced a resurrection. We were by nature 'dead in trespasses and sins', but God, 'who is rich in mercy', came and granted spiritual life to us (Eph. 2:1,4-5). The apostle Paul also attributes this resurrection to the power of God. He speaks of 'the exceeding greatness of his power toward us who believe' (Eph. 1:19).

Christians also have another resurrection coming. The Lord Jesus Christ will some day return from heaven to receive his people unto himself. The apostle Paul writes, 'For the Lord himself will descend from heaven with a shout, with the voice of an archangel, and with the trumpet of God. And the dead in Christ will rise first' (1 Thess. 4:16).

On that day the bodies of all the dead saints will be raised from their graves and joined once more to their souls which went to be with the Lord at the time of death. Living saints will be caught up to meet the Lord in the air. And there, in the midst of that vast throng, each saint will realize more fully than ever before what a marvel it is that he or she should have been made an object of the saving mercy and power of God.

Those who participate in that happy occasion will do so only on the basis of the redeeming work of Christ. If we want to celebrate the mercy and power of God on that day, we must repent of our sins and place our faith and trust in Christ. He, and he alone, is the channel through whom the saving mercy and power of God flow to undeserving sinners.

7.
The Lord provides for the needs of his people

Please read 2 Kings 4:38-44

These verses present us with two more miracles performed by Elisha. Like the two immediately preceding them, these miracles show God's Word breaking into apparently hopeless situations to provide for the needs of his people. Taken together, the four miracles of 2 Kings 4 are a splendid demonstration of how the Lord met the everyday needs of his faithful people in a time rife with apostasy and idolatry. The sufficiency of the Lord flowed to his faithful remnant through the word of Elisha the prophet.

God's people still look to the Word of God for sustaining strength in the midst of difficult and harrowing circumstances. The Bible is an unfailing source of comfort for faithful men and women who have come to the end of their resources. F. W. Krummacher says, 'It shows what God is to His children in seasons of difficulty and distress.'[1]

The captives in Babylon, very conscious of being a small remnant, would have found substantial consolation in being reminded by these miracles of the sufficiency of their God.

The miracle of purified food (4:38-41)

In setting the stage for the miracle of the stew, the author tells us that it occurred at Gilgal (4:38), the point of departure for Elisha and Elijah before the latter was translated (2:1-2). The author supplies additional background by pointing out the time of the miracle — that is, during a famine (4:38). Those who regard this as an unnecessary miracle seem to forget this vital detail: every scrap of food was precious at that time, and lost food was a tragedy of immense proportions.

The famine was so severe that the school of prophets in this area was forced to take innovative measures just to eat. Vegetation that would not normally be eaten might serve very well if it were part of a stew. So while Elisha's servant fetched some water to boil, the young prophets went scavenging for things to fill the pot. It was a catch-as-catch-can proposition.

One young prophet came upon **'a wild vine'** and gathered from it **'a lapful of wild gourds'**. The young man must have felt very good about what he had discovered. He and the other prophets could not identify these gourds (4:39), but they looked good and probably would look even better when they were added to the stew. So in they went! Matthew Henry humorously concludes that the sons of the prophets '... were better skilled in divinity than in natural philosophy, and read their Bibles more than their herbals'.[2]

As Adam and Eve learned in the Garden of Eden, that which is appealing to the eye may in fact bring terrible harm (Gen. 3:6-19). So it was here. The stew looked good, and it no doubt smelled good, but it was not good. After tasting it, the young prophets cried out to Elisha: **'Man of God, there is death in the pot!'** (4:40).

The stew could have been thrown away, but Elisha would not have his students go hungry. He commanded that flour be thrown into the pot, and the stew became good. The means that Elisha used to perform this miracle seems to be utterly absurd and foolish. Flour cast into stew would in the normal course of events have no efficacy whatsoever, but by this apparently foolish means the stew was purified. F. W. Krummacher writes, 'Thus a handful of meal in the hand of the Almighty sufficed to disarm death, to disappoint hell, to preserve the salt of the earth, and to sustain His church in the world. Let none be afraid who have the God of Jacob for their help.'[3]

God has always delighted in accomplishing his ends through instruments the world considers foolish and absurd. When the giant Goliath was menacing the army of Israel, God used David, his sling and five stones to slay the giant and effect Israel's deliverance. The supreme example of this is, of course, the cross of Christ. On the basis of that apparently foolish cross, God redeems polluted sinners, just as he purified polluted stew.

The miracle of multiplied food (4:42-44)

The author turns from the miracle of the stew to another related to food. A man from Baal Shalisha gave **'twenty loaves of barley bread, and newly ripened grain'** (4:42) to Elisha.

A picture of the godly remnant

It is significant that this man came from 'Baal Shalisha' ('lord of Shalisha'), a centre of worship for one of the many Canaanite deities or Baals. He came to the prophet Elisha in compliance with the law of Moses which required that grain offerings be given to the priests of Israel (Lev. 2:14; 23:9-21; Num. 18:13; Deut. 18:4-5). R. L. Hubbard notes that this gift to Elisha required the man to bypass 'in protest the apostate northern religious leaders at the sanctuary nearby at Bethel'.[4]

This man serves as a reminder of the godly remnant in Israel. Although idolatry and apostasy were flourishing, God still had his people who remained faithful and who appreciated the godly ministry of the prophet Elisha.

No matter how evil may increase and prosper, it will never succeed in eradicating the work of the Lord. God has always had, and will continue to have, his faithful people. He never leaves himself without the testimony of faithful people.

A miscalculation

The man from Baal Shalisha apparently thought his gift would be sufficient for the prophet to feed those in his school, but he soon learned that Elisha's school was larger than he had realized.

Elisha's servant, who received the gift, could have used some schooling in delicacy and diplomacy. Instead of thanking the man for his generosity, he focused on the inadequacy of the gift: **'What? Shall I set this before one hundred men?'** (4:43). The servant appears to have held the view that the gift could not be used at all because it was not enough!

The power of God's Word

Elisha was again present to redeem the situation. He intervened with these words: **'Give it to the people, that they may eat; for thus says the LORD: ' "They shall eat and have some left over" '** (4:43). The food was distributed and the promise was realized. The miracle showed the power of the Word of God and its sufficiency for the needs of God's people.

Elisha's miracle, astounding as it was, cannot compare with our Lord's use of meagre supplies to feed five thousand on one occasion and four thousand on another (Mark 6:35-44; 8:1-10). In each of those instances, food was left over, as it was after the members of Elisha's school had been fed.

The God of the miracles

The miracles of the Lord are intended to point us to the God of the miracles. We are to look beyond them to the Lord himself. The miracles of the purified stew and the multiplied food drive us to draw three conclusions.

1. God is real and living

We may rest assured that the men who made up Elisha's school of the prophets needed this reminder. They must have often grown discouraged as they witnessed Israel's continued interest in Baal and their devotion to the cult of Jeroboam. But these miracles powerfully and decisively demonstrated that their God was alive and well. The prophets were reminded that he had the power to defeat all false gods, and they must have concluded that in his own time and way he would do so.

Our own times are so filled with militant paganism and idolatry that we might very well find our spirits sinking. Let us take heart! The God of Elisha is still alive and his power is not diminished.

2. God can do the impossible

Sceptics dismiss these miracles as being impossible. Yes, the things Elisha did were impossible. That is the point. What is impossible to us is not to God. Gabriel clearly stated this when he visited a young woman named Mary to announce that she would conceive and bear a son while she was still a virgin. Mary's question was perfectly logical: 'How can this be, since I do not know a man?' (Luke 1:34). And Gabriel answered, 'For with God nothing will be impossible' (Luke 1:37).

3. God has genuine compassion for human need

To have compassion is to feel pity or sympathy for those who are distressed. We may rest assured that while Elisha himself was a compassionate man, his miracles reflect the far greater compassion of God.

We need look no further than the ministry of our Lord Jesus Christ to see the compassion of God. Jesus was God in human flesh. If he was compassionate, God is compassionate. And there can be no doubt that Jesus was compassionate. Compassion was the hallmark of his life and ministry (Matt. 9:35-36; 14:14; 15:32; Mark 10:21; Luke 7:13).

The compassion of Jesus was such that Matthew was able to assert that he fulfilled this Old Testament prophecy:

A bruised reed he will not break,
And smoking flax he will not quench...

(Matt. 12:20).

The greatest example of the compassion of Jesus came, of course, when he went to the cross to make atonement for his people.

The compassion of Jesus did not end on the cross. It is an ongoing and continuous reality in the lives of his people. The author of Hebrews took notice of this with these words: 'Seeing then that we have a great High Priest who has passed through the heavens, Jesus the Son of God, let us hold fast our confession. For we do not have a High Priest who cannot sympathize with our weaknesses...' (Heb. 4:14-15).

The context of the miracles

The two miracles recorded in this passage occurred within the framework of a school of the prophets. The prophets who were in exile with the captives and ministered to them must have found these episodes to be of keen interest. In each case someone was working for the Lord's cause only to see his labour tainted or diminished in some way. But failure was not the final word because the prophet Elisha stepped into each situation to retrieve or redeem it. The miracles he performed unite their voices to declare this soul-cheering truth: labour for the Lord is not in vain. The apostle Paul states the same truth in these words: 'Therefore, my beloved brethren, be steadfast, immovable, always abounding in the work of the Lord, knowing that your labour is not in vain in the Lord' (1 Cor. 15:58).

The young prophets of Elisha's day needed this truth. Discouragement in the Lord's work must have often run high among them. The twin perils of Baal and Bethel continued to threaten the nation of Israel. Wickedness abounded on every hand. All the while the storm clouds of judgement continued to gather.

Christians today need this truth no less than those young prophets. Our own time mass-produces discouragement for the people of God in general and for ministers in particular. There is real help for all discouraged saints in Elisha's miracles among the prophets.

When our labour is marred

One wonders how the young prophet felt when he discovered that his gourds ruined the stew. He had tried to be helpful, but he had failed. How happy he would have been when Elisha's miracle made the stew edible — with his gourds still in it! The purification of the stew points us ahead to that time when God will finally redeem all creation from the ravages of sin by creating a new heaven and a new earth (Rom. 8:18-25; Rev. 21:1-4).

But Elisha redeemed more than the stew. He also redeemed the labour of the young prophet. How very encouraging this is for every minister of the gospel! Our very best efforts are always tarnished and weakened by our failures. We do not serve the Lord perfectly. We do not preach his gospel perfectly. Our service and our preaching always have harmful gourds in them. But the Lord graciously overrules our gourds and uses our ministries to save souls and to strengthen the saints. And, one glorious day, he will finally say to every faithful saint, 'Well done, good and faithful servant; you were faithful over a few things, I will make you ruler over many things. Enter into the joy of your lord' (Matt. 25:21,23).

When our labour is insufficient

We must again note that Elisha did more than provide food for the school of the prophets. Just as he had redeemed the labour of the prophet who gathered the gourds, so he now redeems the labour of the man from Baal Shalisha. This man's labour was not adequate as it was presented, but Elisha made it adequate.

Every minister of the gospel knows his labour is not adequate for the task he faces. No one has sufficient gifts for the saving of souls, no matter how great his intellect or how eloquent his tongue. But we must not allow our insufficiency to drive us from the task because it pleases God to overrule it. He is pleased to take up our feeble efforts and send along with them the regenerating work of his Spirit so that people are truly saved through our ministries. He assures us that while we, his ministers, are inadequate, we carry in Scripture a powerful word (Isa. 55:10-11; Heb. 4:12). Even earthen vessels can carry glorious treasures. God has designed it in this way so that 'the excellence of the power may be of God and not of us' (2 Cor. 4:7).

8.
Naaman in the grip of grace

Please read 2 Kings 5:1-15

With this passage the author continues his emphasis on the miracles of Elisha. Here he leaves the context of the school of the prophets to relate the miraculous healing of Naaman, a Syrian captain.

The original readers of 2 Kings may very well have been perplexed about the author's inclusion of this episode. With this narrative the author continues developing the story of Elisha, but why should he go out of his way to lay so much emphasis on a miracle for a Syrian captain? We shall see. But let's think about Naaman now as a recipient of God's grace.

The stages of Naaman's experience

The account enables us to follow Naaman through four major stages.

1. Haughty

When we first meet Naaman he seems likeable enough. He, the **'commander of the army of the king of Syria'**, is further identified as **'a great and honourable man in the eyes**

of his master, because by him the LORD had given victory to Syria' (5:1).

But we soon see that Naaman was a very proud man. His furious rage outside Elisha's house and his assertion of the superior qualities of the rivers of Syria (5:11-12) put his pride on display. Naaman was filled with nationalistic pride. Syria meant everything to him. He undoubtedly loved her military prowess and his part in it, her religion and her culture. He loved his own station in life and attributed that to the greatness of Syria.

In his book *Elijah and Elisha*, Ronald S. Wallace writes, 'Naaman the Syrian is living in our midst today. We call him "the man of the world". He is an interesting and in many ways admirable type of man. He has a real zest for life. He fully enjoys the best of all this world can offer him in culture, amusement, wealth, variety, pomp and sport. But the religion of the Bible is to him something cold and unreal compared with all of this. He sees little to glory in in the Cross of Christ compared with what he has in the realm of the world. He feels that the Kingdom of God is a distant and very unattractive affair compared with the kingdoms of this world... From his own point of view, the "man of the world" feels quite certain that his way of life is vastly superior to that of the man who confines most of his life to the sphere of the Church... After all, if we are going to measure value and worth of life by the amount of excitement and colour and beauty, amusement and adventure it offers us, then it is not really of any advantage to become a Christian.'[1]

2. Helpless

We may picture Naaman proceeding very happily down life's pathway as he enjoyed his culture and what it offered him. Then one dreadful day everything suddenly changed. Naaman was diagnosed as suffering from leprosy, the most dreaded disease of his time. Wallace pointedly says, 'Syria gave Naaman up when he became a leper. It could give him birth, feed him, educate him, tickle his fancy and amuse him. It could pipe to him while he danced and fill his life with gaiety and variety — but it could not wash him clean. Syria had done in one way far more for Naaman than the land of Israel could ever have done for any of its children — but it could not wash him clean!'[2]

3. Humbled

A bright ray of light suddenly breaks in upon Naaman's ashen sky. A young girl whom he had seized in Israel and brought home to serve his wife offers this note of hope to Naaman's wife: **'If only my master were with the prophet who is in Samaria! For he would heal him of his leprosy'** (5:3). This glad word begins a process of humbling. Powerful, proud Naaman receives instruction from a mere child — and not even a Syrian child!

Naaman quickly attempts to put the matter into the realm with which he is at ease. He goes to his king, who agrees to write a letter to the King of Israel (5:4-5). He amasses a very impressive gift (5:5). This is Naaman's world. He is taking action and making things happen. The slave girl had specifically identified the prophet Elisha as Naaman's hope, but Naaman's pride will not permit him to deal with a lowly prophet.

Naaman's strategy, however, all comes to nought. The King of Israel reads the letter from the King of Syria and is beside himself with despair: **'Am I God, to kill and make alive, that this man sends a man to me to heal him of his leprosy? Therefore please consider, and see how he seeks a quarrel with me'** (5:7). Naaman's desire to keep the matter buttoned up among the movers and shakers of the day is shattered. The King of Israel proves to be as helpless in the face of the leprosy as Naaman himself.

At this point Elisha intervenes by sending this message to the King of Israel: **'Why have you torn your clothes? Please let him come to me, and he shall know that there is a prophet in Israel'** (5:8).

Naaman has run out of options. He has to go to the prophet, but he will only go on his own terms. He still has his **'ten talents of silver, six thousand shekels of gold, and ten changes of clothing'** (5:5). He will at least have the satisfaction of paying for his healing, even if he must receive it from a prophet. And he consoles himself with the thought that the Israelite prophet will certainly take into account the fact that he is dealing with a great man.

Naaman is driven from this refuge as well. Elisha does not even take the trouble to come out and greet him, but instead sends him this message: **'Go and wash in the Jordan seven times, and your flesh shall be restored to you, and you shall be clean'** (5:10). This is the last straw! Naaman refuses to be humbled any further! The prophet has not done as Naaman had pictured. He has not come out to perform a dignified ceremony. Alexander Maclaren splendidly observes that Naaman wanted to be treated like a great man who happened to be a leper, but Elisha's cure treated him as a leper who happened to be a great man.[3]

And the cure the prophet has proposed is out of the question. Naaman is not prepared to bathe in the muddy water of Jordan when he has perfectly good rivers back home. If it was a matter of bathing in a river, Naaman would choose his own river!

Naaman cuts quite a figure in these verses. He is helpless in the dreaded grip of leprosy and a cure is made available, but his pride will not allow him to accept the cure. He goes away in a rage (5:12).

4. Healed

Naaman did not realize it, but he was in the grip of God's grace. When God takes hold of a man, he doesn't let go. God never lacks instruments to do his work of grace. Naaman's blind and furious rage was powerless to defeat God's purpose. Naaman had servants with him, servants whom God would use. They waited for the most furious part of Naaman's wrath to burn itself out and then respectfully approached him: **'My father, if the prophet had told you to do something great, would you not have done it? How much more then, when he says to you, "Wash, and be clean"?'** (5:13). This word was so sensible and disarming. Naaman's disease was so very dreadful and health so very desirable that he would not have hesitated to do 'something great' had the prophet required it. Why should he refuse to do something simple?

At this point Naaman capitulated. He needed healing. Syria could not help him. His wealth and dignity could not help him. He would heed the message of Elisha and do as he said. To the Jordan river he went, and there, after his seventh washing, his flesh was **'restored like the flesh of a little child'** (5:14).

Some lessons from Naaman's experience

A message of encouragement

We must frequently remind ourselves of the pastoral nature of 2 Kings. The author wrote to help his people who were in captivity in Babylon. He wrote to explain why they were there and to keep their faith alive. The original readers undoubtedly understood and appreciated this. But, as we noted earlier, they may have also been somewhat perplexed over his inclusion of this particular account. Here Naaman, a Syrian captain, is healed of leprosy. With this narrative the author continues developing the story of Elisha, but why should he go out of his way to lay so much emphasis on a miracle performed for a Syrian captain?

A little reflection may very well have caused these readers to appreciate the profound significance of this miracle. The God who had the power to redeem Naaman from his leprosy certainly had the power to redeem their nation from Babylon. These captives also had to be encouraged: 'Exiles were troubled over their separation from the land of Israel. Could they worship God in a strange land?'[4] The experience of Naaman gave a resounding 'yes' to that question because it showed that God is not limited by national boundaries.

A message about personal faith

The story of Naaman also took the captives to a central truth about God's covenant with Israel. How often the people of Israel lost track of this! God's election of Israel did not mean that nationality itself was enough to put a person in a right relationship with God. It was not mere descent from Abraham that brought an individual into the covenant, but sharing the faith of Abraham (Rom. 4:11,16; Gal. 3:29). On the one hand, it was possible for a non-Israelite such as Naaman to come to faith in the God of Israel. On the other hand, it was possible for Israelites after the flesh to miss out on that faith.

We do not enter the kingdom in groups but only as individuals with a true and living faith.

A message about the sovereignty of God's grace

Because physical descent was never the very essence of the covenant, God was not obligated to restrict his grace only to the people of Israel. He could and did reach beyond Israel to save Gentiles. The Lord Jesus himself would later say, 'And many lepers were in Israel in the time of Elisha the prophet, and none of them was cleansed except Naaman the Syrian' (Luke 4:27). It was not a shortage of lepers in Israel that caused God to grant healing to Naaman. It was because God, in sovereign grace, chose to heal Naaman. Salvation is always a matter of the grace of God.

The conversion of Ruth (Ruth 1:15-18) and that of the Ninevites (Jonah 3:5-10) are two examples of God reaching out in grace to Gentiles. They also serve as a wonderful anticipation of the great gathering of Gentiles into God's kingdom after the death of the Lord Jesus.

A message about responsibility

The captives in Babylon could learn from the slave girl that they were to be witnesses to God's grace in the midst of their circumstances. She could have allowed the difficulty of her situation and bitterness towards her captors to overwhelm her. She could have kept the word of truth about Elisha to herself. But she spoke that word and Naaman was blessed. Daniel serves as another example on this matter. He looked upon his captivity in Babylon as an opportunity to serve God and to speak for God. He made Babylon his mission-field.

The apostle Paul also shines as a remarkable example for us. Instead of bemoaning one of his episodes of imprisonment, he rejoiced that the Lord had used it for 'the furtherance of the gospel' (Phil. 1:12). The fact that he closed his epistle by referring to the saints in Caesar's household indicates that Paul had used his imprisonment to witness to his guards (Phil. 4:22).

Let us learn from these examples to look upon every circumstance, no matter how trying, as an avenue to blessing and usefulness and not a dead end.

A message about submitting to God and his gospel

Naaman's experience speaks to us at yet another level — that is, the need to humble ourselves before the gospel message. Multitudes are following the path taken by Naaman when he was unwilling to submit to Elisha's instructions.

The Bible tells us we are all afflicted with the dreadful, deadly disease of sin, a disease which is even more deadly than Naaman's leprosy because it ultimately issues in eternal destruction. The Bible also tells us there is absolutely no cure for sin except through divine intervention. But, wonder of wonders, the Bible also says God has intervened and made a cure available in and through the person of his Son, Jesus Christ. This Christ, by his perfect life and his atoning death, has done all that is necessary for our sins to be forgiven and for us to have eternal life in heaven.

This is incredibly glorious good news, but, amazingly enough, there are multitudes who do as Naaman did. After hearing this good news, they turn away! It's not that they don't need a cure for sin. They do! And it's not that a cure is not available. It is!

Why, then, do so many turn away from the cure? The answer is that the gospel offends them. It violates their wisdom and their dignity. It doesn't take into account their riches, social standing, or education. It says all without exception are in sin, and it further says there is nothing we can do to earn or deserve salvation. We are entirely dependent on the grace of God. We want to come before God with Naaman's shekels and changes of clothing, and have him accept us on the basis of who we are and what we have done. But just as Elisha ignored Naaman's wealth and dignity, so God refuses all our attempts to stand before him on the basis of our own merits or accomplishments.

Furthermore, the gospel requires that we do something that seems ludicrous and repugnant. It tells us we must bow in repentance and faith before Jesus' atoning death on the cross. This offends many. They look at that bloody cross and find themselves thinking there must be another way, a way that is more sophisticated and appealing. They, like Naaman, have no trouble thinking of other things that make more sense, but the finger of God points unrelentingly at that cross as the one and only way of salvation.

No generation has been more impressed with human wisdom and dignity than our own. This is not to say there is not a legitimate place for this emphasis. We are all made in the image of God, and this does indeed give every human being a basic dignity and provides the basis for human rights. But the proper place for emphasizing human dignity is in our relationship to others, not in our relationship to God. Human dignity is fine among human beings, but it is insufficient when it comes to standing before the Lord. Our dignity comes from God, but we must never use it as an excuse for not bowing before him. Many have trouble making this distinction, and when the gospel confronts them with its demand for submission the spirit of Naaman can easily come to life in them.

When Naaman made his way back to the prophet, things were different. This time Elisha saw him. And this time Naaman, instead of saying, 'I thought,' says, **'I know…'** He says, **'Indeed, now I know that there is no God in all the earth, except in Israel…'** (5:15). 'What a great lesson there is here! If we ever want to be able to say "I know," we have got to stop saying, "I thought". In other words, if we ever want to have the joy and the peace and the confidence the gospel brings, we must stop arguing with God and accept the gospel as the only cure for sin. We must stop standing on our dignity and our wisdom and bow before the wisdom of God in Christ Jesus.'[5]

9.
Two examples of spiritual realities

Please read 2 Kings 5:16-27

These verses continue the story of Naaman the Syrian. They also set before us the sad and tragic end of Gehazi, the servant of Elisha.

This chapter has leprosy at its very centre. It opens with Naaman being a leper, moves on to record his cure and closes with Gehazi becoming a leper. For Gehazi there was no cure. But there is much more to this chapter than leprosy. That horrible affliction is emblematic of spiritual truths and conditions that are just as real today as the leprosy suffered by both Naaman and Gehazi was then.

It was the cure of Naaman's leprosy that led him to true faith in God. Hear his sparkling confession of faith after he was cured: 'Indeed, now I know that there is no God in all the earth, except in Israel...' (5:15). Gehazi's leprosy, on the other hand, came about because of his spiritual condition. We look at these two men, then, for insight and instruction about spiritual realities.

The conversion of Naaman

We look to Naaman as an example of one who was truly converted to faith in God. We can say Naaman was truly converted because he followed up his heartfelt confession of faith with evidences of a changed life. There are many who make a profession of faith but never show any indication of change. Naaman was not one of these.

The very fact that his confession of faith was uttered to Elisha the prophet speaks volumes. Only a short time before this Naaman had left Elisha's house in a rage. He was indignant that the prophet had not come out to see him and that he had required him to wash in the muddy water of the Jordan river (5:11-12). But after he was cured, his attitude towards the prophet was entirely different. It is always so. No sinner ever comes to the saving knowledge of God without feeling a profound sense of gratitude for those who faithfully proclaimed the gospel to him.

We also note that Naaman now had an unrelenting desire to worship the God who had so graciously healed him. He made two requests of Elisha. First, he asked for two mule-loads of earth so he could build an altar to the Lord in his own land, the land of Syria (5:17). Secondly, he asked that Elisha pardon him for bowing down in the house of the false god Rimmon (5:18). These two requests pose serious challenges to commentators.

Naaman and Israelite soil

One problem has to do with Naaman's request for Israelite soil. Was this not a superstitious belief that was out of keeping with his new-found faith? We may say that it was, but in doing so we must also make allowance for the fact that Naaman was a new convert. We should not expect him at this point to have a full and mature understanding of the things of God. Joseph Hall notes: 'It is not for us to expect a full stature in the cradle of conversion. As nature, so grace rises, by many degrees, to perfection. Leprosy was in Naaman cured at once, not corruption.'[1]

Naaman and the house of Rimmon

A second problem has to do with his request for Elisha's pardon for bowing in the house of Rimmon. There seems to be a glaring contradiction here. With one breath, Naaman maintains that he will no longer serve idols (5:17). With the next breath, he apparently anticipates going into the temple of an idol (5:18).

How are we to explain this? Some commentators resolve the problem by suggesting that the words of verse 18 are properly translated in this way: 'Yet in this thing may the LORD pardon your servant: when my master *went* into the temple of Rimmon to worship there, and he *leaned* on my hand, and I *bowed* down in the temple of Rimmon — when I *bowed* down in the temple of Rimmon, may the LORD please pardon your servant in this thing' (5:18). Those who hold this view believe, then, that Naaman was asking Elisha to pardon him for being an idolater in the past.

Others accept the present tense and think Naaman was merely apprising Elisha of the reality that he would be facing once he returned to Syria. He knew there would be occasions when the king would compel him to go into the house of Rimmon, but he wanted the prophet to know that on those occasions he would not consent with his heart to the worship conducted there.

Elisha's acquiescence

A third problem with these verses has to do with the complicity of Elisha in all this. He did not rebuke Naaman for requesting Israelite soil, nor did he rebuke him for saying he would go into the house of Rimmon. Should Elisha not have told him that Israelite soil was not necessary to worship the Lord in a way that is pleasing to him? Should Elisha not have told him to stay out of the house of Rimmon even if it cost him his position? Instead Elisha merely said to him, **'Go in peace'** (5:19).

Elisha may appear to have compromised at this point, but in reality he was trusting Naaman and his spiritual development to the same grace of God that had converted him. He knew that grace would continue to work in Naaman to bring him to maturity and to wise judgement on difficult issues.

We must also give due weight to Naaman's particular circumstances — that is, the fact that he was living under the Old Covenant. C. F. Keil offers this word of explanation: 'Under the old covenant the time had not yet come in which the heathen could be required to break off from all their heathen ways, unless they would formally enter into fellowship with the covenant nation.'[2]

The thing we must not do is let the difficulties of interpretation obscure Naaman's genuine desire to worship God, a desire which shows that he had come to faith. Where there is no such desire there is no faith. What are we to make, then, of those who claim to know God but habitually absent themselves from worship? Are they not terribly deceived?

The hypocrisy of Gehazi

The issue of deception comes out in the account of Gehazi. We have in him an example of one who appeared to belong to God but did not. In other words, Naaman was the outsider who came in, while Gehazi was the insider who went out. Gehazi went out because he never understood the grace of God.

Here is the story. After being healed of his leprosy, Naaman had offered to give Elisha the wealth he had brought along (5:5,15). But Elisha had refused and sent him on his way

(5:16,19). Naaman must understand that his cure was not something that he had earned or deserved. It was entirely of the grace of God.

Gehazi had a different view. After Naaman left the premises, he pursued him and pretended that his master, Elisha, had experienced a change of heart and now wanted some of the goods Naaman had brought (5:22). In reality, Gehazi wanted the goods for himself.

Gehazi should have known that his ruse would not work. He had been associated with Elisha long enough to know that the prophet was in touch with the God from whom nothing is hidden. Sure enough, when Gehazi returned from his ill-conceived venture, Elisha was waiting for him with a devastating announcement: **'Therefore the leprosy of Naaman shall cling to you and your descendants for ever'** (5:27).

Why was Gehazi treated so severely? What was wrong with what he did? Terence E. Fretheim offers this explanation: 'The issue at stake for Elisha is more than the deception or greed. The phrase "is this a time?" (5:26) suggests that the issue is the possible effect Gehazi's behaviour may have on Naaman... There may be "a time" to speak in terms of gifts to be offered, but right now the grace of God needs to fill Naaman's vision and the freedom of the life of faith needs to be reinforced. Gehazi's sin is, finally, a *theological* sin, for it endangers the very nature of faith and obscures the gracious work of God'[3] (italics are his).

Gehazi stands, then, as another in a long series of examples of severe temporal judgement that was intended and designed to drive home a crucial spiritual truth. The truth in this case is that salvation is always a matter of the grace of God.

The severe temporal judgement that befell Gehazi serves as a picture in miniature of the eternal judgement that will befall all those who deny that grace. The supreme tragedy of Gehazi is that he denied that grace as one who seemed to have understood it. Ronald S. Wallace writes, 'But Gehazi was not content in Israel. He could not understand Elisha for letting pass this wonderful opportunity of enrichment from Syria. To him it was nothing more than sheer stupidity and narrow-minded principle that had kept Elisha from taking such a gift. And now Gehazi, perhaps for the first time in his life, knew where his heart was. His heart was not in Israel. He had to live and work there certainly. Indeed he had to do his job at the very centre of its religious life, but his heart was not in the service of the God of Israel. His heart was in the gold and silver and silk that he had seen Naaman pack up and throw back in his chariot as if it were mere rubbish. His heart was in the land that could produce and display all that. And having caught a glimpse of what Syria could offer he was even less content with what Israel could give him. Gehazi was maddened by the thought that Elisha had been offered a chance of having a little bit of Syria in Israel and had refused it and now Naaman was taking back a little bit of Israel to Syria!'[4]

Yes, it is sadly possible to be counted among the people of God and never have truly embraced the grace of God that brings salvation. Gehazi was a man who in some ways resembled Judas Iscariot in the New Testament, a man who was blessed with enormous spiritual privileges but never saw the heart of the matter. Gehazi saw God at work in the prophet Elisha and undoubtedly heard clear and powerful teaching from the prophet's lips, but he never came to understand that sinners can stand before God only on the basis of what God does for them and not on the basis of what they do for God.

We can go still further. Because he was so closely associated with the ministerial office, we can also say that Gehazi represents all ministers who distort the gospel message of grace by teaching that sinners can be saved by their own efforts. The true gospel minister removes all other grounds of hope from sinners and teaches them to say:

Nothing in my hand I bring,
Simply to thy cross I cling.

A message for the captives

Gehazi had to decide whether he was going to be an Israelite
or a Syrian. He chose the latter. The captives in Babylon were
in a similar situation, one that demanded that they determine
whether they were going to be Israelites or Babylonians. The
book of Daniel documents the efforts of the Babylonians to
'Babylonianize' Daniel and his friends. Those men could have
become like Gehazi, but they did not. Their hearts were so
firmly attached to Israel that they could not embrace Babylon.

Like the captives, we also live in a culture that screams for
our submission, and the question ever before each of us is
this: 'Where is my heart?'

10.
Another miracle among the prophets

Please read 2 Kings 6:1-7

These verses report yet another miracle performed by Elisha in the context of the school of the prophets. We can assume that Elisha was much devoted to the spiritual nurture and training of these young men and that they were much devoted to him.

This miracle, like many of the others performed by Elisha, dealt with everyday life. But while it helped an ordinary man engaged in an ordinary task, the miracle itself is ablaze with spiritual truth and meaning.

The account of this miracle falls quite naturally into two major parts: the setting for the miracle and the miracle itself.

The setting for the miracle (6:1-4)

The building project (6:1-2)

Idolatry was flourishing in the land of Israel. It is only as we keep this context in mind that we can appreciate what the sons of the prophets had to say to Elisha: **'See now, the place where we dwell with you is too small for us'** (6:1).

There have been many times in which evil was so very strong and virulent that it appeared as if the Lord's cause would entirely fail. Elisha's predecessor, Elijah, had experienced such a time. After Jezebel threatened to take his life, he fled to Mt Horeb, the mountain on which Moses had received the law of God for Israel. Mt Horeb was the place where it all began, and Elijah went back to report that it had all ended. He, and he alone, was left and his life was hanging by a thread (1 Kings 19:10). Elijah was in for a surprise. It was not over. The Lord had reserved seven thousand faithful ones in Israel who had refused to bow the knee to Baal (1 Kings 19:18).

The captives in Babylon may very well have thought that their nation had reached the end of the line, that Israel would become assimilated into Babylon and never exist again as a nation. The fact that the school of prophets had to build larger quarters in an evil time was a tiny reminder for them that God preserves his cause even in dark and evil times.

The presence of the prophet (6:3-4)

The desire of the prophets for Elisha's company

One of the young prophets, undoubtedly speaking for the whole group, said to Elisha, **'Please consent to go with your servants'** (6:3).

On the surface it appears to be of no real significance that the young prophets desired Elisha to accompany them. We might even be inclined to chalk it up to their being mannerly and polite. But if we understand that Elisha represented the Word of God to these men, we must say that their invitation was not due to their observing a social amenity. It was rather an expression of their delight in the Word of God.

This delight in Elisha, the bearer of the Word of God, put them, as we shall soon see, in the way of blessing. What blessings might we receive if we would make it our practice to take the Word of God with us in every situation and circumstance of life?

The desire of the prophets to have Elisha with them may very well have constituted a stinging reminder to the captives that their present plight was due to their failure to delight themselves in the Word of God. Perhaps those captives also heard in this note a resounding plea for them to delight in that Word while they were in captivity.

The interest of Elisha in their endeavours

The presence of Elisha with these young prophets also indicates something of his interest in them and their endeavours. The prophet through whom the Lord had worked stunning miracles did not allow himself to be puffed up with pride. He did not consider himself to be of such importance that he could not associate with these men in such a mundane activity as constructing a new building.

As the Lord's representative, Elisha's willingness to be involved with this project pictures for us the Lord's interest in those details we consider to be small and insignificant. The Lord Jesus himself assures us of this with these words: 'Look at the birds of the air, for they neither sow nor reap nor gather into barns; yet your heavenly Father feeds them. Are you not of more value than they?' (Matt. 6:26).

The prophet Isaiah anticipated that the captives in Babylon would feel as if they had been removed from God's radar screen:

Why do you say, O Jacob,
And speak, O Israel:
'My way is hidden from the LORD,
And my just claim is passed over by my God'?
(Isa. 40:27).

The prophet proceeded to announce that God, 'the Creator of the ends of the earth' (Isa. 40:28), would not only take note of them in Babylon but would actually strengthen them there (Isa. 40:29-31).

The miracle itself (6:5-7)

While the prophets were engaged in their work, one of them suddenly saw his axe-head fly off the handle and fall into the muddy water of the Jordan river.

The young prophet was very distressed. So poor that he could not buy an axe for himself, he had begged one from someone else. Now it was gone, and he had no way of replacing it. Those who have borrowed books from the church library which they have not yet returned would do well to learn from the distress of this young man!

The situation looked hopeless, but it wasn't. No sooner had the axe-head hit the water than the young prophet cried out to Elisha: **'Alas master! For it was borrowed'** (6:5). The prophet immediately took the situation in hand. He threw a stick into the very place where the axe-head had disappeared, and the iron head rose to the surface (6:6).

Raymond B. Dillard writes, 'Remember that the ancient Canaanites viewed Judge River and Prince Sea as rivals of Baal who threatened to overwhelm and destroy him. But here God shows again that the waters do not threaten him — rather, they do his bidding. The cosmos cannot be a rival to God, for he has created it and he rules over it to do his own good will.'[1]

Some have tried to explain this episode in a naturalistic way. They say that Elisha merely peered into the murky waters of the Jordan, saw the axe-head lying there, inserted a long stick into the opening and lifted it to the surface. But the account says nothing of the sort. It tells us that the stick was thrown into the water and that the axe-head was not lifted but floated to the surface. The result was that the axe-head was restored to the prophet, and he was able to resume his work.

The encouragement of the miracle

Comfort for the captives

The story of the recovered axe-head must have been a source of much comfort to the first readers of 2 Kings. Was there a future for their nation? Would the promises of God regarding their nation and the coming Messiah ever be fulfilled? Many probably thought all was hopeless, but the God who made iron float could make their nation live again and send the Messiah.

Comfort for the prophets in captivity

The prophets who were with the captives in Babylon probably found that the story of the recovered axe-head, like the accounts of the purified stew and the multiplied food (4:38-44), had a particular relevance for them. When his axe-head fell into the water, the young prophet must have considered it, and the labour he could do with it, hopelessly lost. When Elisha recovered the axe-head, he simultaneously redeemed the labour of the young man. What an encouragement it must have been for the prophets in exile to apply this account to their own situation! It encouraged them to believe that their labour for the Lord in those difficult circumstances was not in vain.

Comfort for the church today

This story should comfort us as well. There have been numerous occasions on which it has appeared that the church has sunk into irretrievable depths, times in which sin and false teachings so abounded that the church herself was overrun with them. God has intervened again and again in such bleak situations to do the work we know as revival.

At the time George Whitefield launched his ministry, evil was having a field day in England. Joseph Butler wrote that scepticism had become so prevalent that Christianity was regard as having been 'discovered to be fictitious ... and nothing remained but to set it up as the subject of mirth and ridicule'.[2] In 1738 Archbishop Thomas Secker referred to a 'torrent of impiety' in the land.[3]

But in those dark and troubled times, England was 'startled by the sound of a voice',[4] the voice of George Whitefield. His voice was joined by those of John and Charles Wesley and others 'in a tremendous chorus of praise and preaching that rang throughout the land'.[5] The result was that, in the words of J. R. Green, '... a religious revival burst forth ... which changed in a few years the whole temper of English society. The Church was restored to life and activity. Religion carried to the hearts of the people a fresh spirit of moral zeal, while it purified our literature and our manners. A new philanthropy reformed our prisons, infused clemency and wisdom into our penal laws, abolished the slave trade, and gave the first impulse to popular education.'[6]

Conditions in the American colonies in 1740 were such that the cause and truth of God appeared as hopelessly lost as the young prophet's sunken axe-head. Iain Murray reports Samuel Blair's assessment of religious conditions in the colonies: 'Religion lay as it were a-dying and ready to expire its last breath of life...'[7] But God once again used George Whitefield to bring a sweeping spiritual awakening. God made the axe-head float!

Every revival of genuine and true religion in seemingly hopeless times is an example of God making the axe-head float. The revivals of the past give us reason to believe that God may very well cause the axe-head to float again!

Comfort for unbelievers

Elisha's recovery of the lost axe-head also conveys a tremendous message of comfort to unbelievers who care to receive it. The truth is that we each come into this world with a nature that was sunken in sin and with absolutely no ability to raise it from that sin. But God graciously lifts sinners to spiritual life and enables them to see their sinful condition and flee to the Lord Jesus Christ who died for sinners (Eph. 2:1-7). God's grace is so great that it lifts dead sinners all the way from the pit of condemnation to the glories of heaven.

Every saint in heaven will be able to say that he was once like the prophet's axe-head — hopelessly lost and unable to help himself — but God graciously raised him.

11.
Ancient messages with abiding value

Please read 2 Kings 6:8-23

These verses show the Lord continuing to use the prophet Elisha. Here the prophet was the means by which God delivered three very important messages, each of which had some connection with the theme of evil.

No theme could be of more interest to the people of God. Evil flourishes to such an extent that we are constantly faced with a number of major temptations. There is the temptation to share in the evil. There is the temptation to be disheartened by the evil. There is the temptation to respond in an evil way to evil-doers. The messages delivered by Elisha the prophet in these verses speak to each of these temptations. These messages lift these verses out of the realm of ancient history and make them live.

The message to the King of Syria (6:8-14,18)

The first of these messages was addressed to the King of Syria. This message may be summarized in this way: avoid the evil of defying God.

The King of Syria learned this the hard way. He essentially thumbed his nose in the face of the God of Israel, only to find himself humiliated. Not wanting to mobilize his whole army and run the risk of losing a decisive battle to Israel, he had resorted to sending raiding parties into Israel. His purpose in doing this was to demoralize and weaken Israel to such an extent that complete conquest would be possible.

While these raids met with initial success, it wasn't long before things began to go sour for the King of Syria. Every time he planned a raid, the Lord informed Elisha of where the Syrians were planning to strike and Elisha informed the King of Israel. Nothing is hidden from God, who sees all and knows all (Job 34:21; Prov. 5:21; 15:3; Jer. 16:17; 32:19).

After several raids failed, the King of Syria became so exasperated that he called in his commanders and accused them of leaking information to Israel (6:11). It was then that he learned that Elisha was the culprit (6:12). Immediately the king dispatched **'horses and chariots and a great army'** (6:14) to Dothan to arrest Elisha and bring him back to Syria. In doing so, the king was essentially defying the God whom Elisha served.

It did not work. Instead of his soldiers capturing Elisha, they themselves were captured. In answer to the prophet's prayer, the Lord blinded the Syrian soldiers (6:18), and the prophet was then able to lead them to the King of Israel in Samaria (6:19-23). Richard Nelson notes: 'This narrative makes the same point as the Book of Kings as a whole. Kings of nations, be they of Judah or Israel, Assyria or even Babylon, were never really in control of the history of God's people. Only God was.'[1]

Defiance of God never works. Centuries before the episode described in these verses, the Philistines thought they could successfully fight against God. They seized the ark of the covenant and put it in the temple of their god, only to see him fall before it and find themselves physically afflicted (1 Sam. 5:1-12).

Many defy God today. They dismiss the teaching that he is the Creator of all things. They deny his government of the universe. They hear of his plan of salvation only to turn away. They scoff at any suggestion that they will have to stand before him in judgement. They may even do this with an air of arrogance and assurance, but this does not make God go away. He assures us that a day is coming in which all the sceptics and scoffers will have to meet him and acknowledge him.

By the way, we may see in the Syrians' focus on Elisha a picture of the way in which Satan and his forces focused on the Lord Jesus Christ during his earthly ministry. But Satan's efforts against Christ did not avail any more than did those of the Syrians against Elisha. In addition to withstanding Satan's temptations in the wilderness, the Lord Jesus Christ dealt the death blow to him and his kingdom by dying on the cross (Col. 2:13-15).

The message to Elisha's servant (6:15-17)

The second person to receive a message from God in this passage is none other than the servant of the prophet Elisha (6:15-17). This message may be stated in these words: the people of God can overcome fear of evil by looking beyond it to the invisible forces of heaven.

The morning after the Syrians encircled the city, Elisha's servant was filled with despair. **'Alas, my master! What shall we do?'**, was his cry to the prophet (6:15).

Elisha calmed his fear by doing two things. He first said, **'Do not fear, for those who are with us are more than those who are with them'** (6:16). After speaking those words, Elisha prayed for the Lord to open the eyes of the servant (6:16), and immediately the young man saw that **'The mountain was full of horses and chariots of fire all around Elisha'** (6:17).

What are we to understand from this? The servant saw nothing less than the hosts of heaven themselves arrayed around Elisha. How small and insignificant the Syrians must have looked in comparison to the heavenly host! Elisha could say, 'Do not fear' (6:16), because there really was nothing to fear. The Syrians were no match for the army of heaven.

What comfort there is for us in what the servant saw! His experience reminds us that there are always two parts to reality, the part we see and the part that is hidden from us. When Elisha's servant looked out on the morning described in this passage he saw Syrians. The Syrians were, of course, there to be seen. They were real. The problem was that the young man saw only Syrians. We Christians often find ourselves in much the same dilemma as Elisha's servant. Evil runs so rampant today that we often feel like throwing up our hands in despair and saying as he did, 'What shall we do?'

His experience tells us that we should look beyond the realities that can be seen to the realities of the spiritual world. It is quite certain that God will never show us these realities in the same way as he did with Elisha's servant, but we can still see them by the eye of faith.

We are called to live as Moses did. We are told that he 'endured as seeing him who is invisible' (Heb. 11:27). Moses faced such hardships and trials that he must often have felt like giving up. But each time he reached that point he was able with the eye of faith to look beyond the here and now to the invisible God (Heb. 11:27), and each time he did so, he received strength to go on.

The apostle Paul followed Moses' example. Here is his testimony: 'Therefore we do not lose heart. Even though our outward man is perishing, yet the inward man is being renewed day by day. For our light affliction, which is but for a moment, is working for us a far more exceeding and eternal weight of glory, while we do not look at the things which are seen, but at the things which are not seen. For the things which are seen are temporary, but the things which are not seen are eternal' (2 Cor. 4:16-18).

How different things are for the unbeliever! He thinks the seen part is all there is, and he governs his life in terms of it. But the Christian knows the unseen part is there, and he refuses to govern his life as though the seen world is all there is.

The message to the King of Israel (6:19-23)

This brings us to the third and final message that God delivered through Elisha, the message to the King of Israel (6:19-23). This message was to overcome evil with good.

While the Syrian soldiers were still blinded, Elisha led them to Samaria where the King of Israel, Jehoram, was. When Jehoram saw the soldiers, he asked Elisha if they should be put to death (6:21).

Elisha responded quickly and decisively: **'You shall not kill them. Would you kill those whom you have taken captive with your sword and your bow? Set food and water before them, that they may eat and drink and go to their master'** (6:22).

John Gill explains Elisha's response in this way: 'When soldiers are made prisoners of war, it is contrary to humanity, to the laws of nature and nations, to kill them in cold blood, and much more those who were not taken by his sword and bow, but by the power and providence of God.'[2]

Elisha's kind response displayed the goodness of God himself to the Syrian soldiers. The goodness of Israel's God took them from death to dining.

What a powerful reminder this is of the redeeming work of Jesus Christ! Because he went to Calvary's cross and there endured the wrath of God in the stead of sinners, there is now no wrath left for them to endure. Instead they will find themselves dining in God's great banquet room (Matt. 8:11). There both Jews and Gentiles will dine together just as they did in Samaria.

While we wait for that wonderful day in heaven, we who know the Lord are to be busy demonstrating his goodness here upon earth. We are to keep this admonition of Paul close to our hearts:

Beloved, do not avenge yourselves, but rather give place to wrath; for it is written, 'Vengeance is mine, I will repay,' says the Lord. Therefore

'If your enemy is hungry, feed him;
If he is thirsty, give him a drink;
For in so doing you will heap coals of fire on his head.'

Do not be overcome by evil, but overcome evil with good

(Rom. 12:19-21).

As we have seen, the original readers of 2 Kings were in captivity in Babylon. They would have had no difficulty at all in seeing the relevance of the three messages presented in these verses.

In the first place, as the King of Syria had defied God, so they and their leaders had defied God by refusing to obey his commandments and by going after idols. Their defiance had now proved to be just as unsuccessful as that of the King of Syria.

Secondly, while they were surrounded by evil in Babylon, there was no need for them to despair. They were also surrounded by the same heavenly host that hovered above Elisha and his servant when they were faced with the Syrians. One captive in Babylon, Daniel, realized this and made this his watchword: 'But there is a God in heaven' (Dan. 2:28). God's people in every generation are called to understand that the real fight is behind the scenes and Christ is the certain victor.

Thirdly, as the King of Israel was to do good to the Syrian soldiers, so the captives were not just to endure their time in Babylon but to witness for God there by doing good. Daniel and his three friends, Meshach, Shadrach and Abed-Nego, serve as wonderful examples of the people of God practising good in a pagan culture.

12.
Timeless responses to crucial messages

Please read 2 Kings 6:24 – 7:20

An interesting cast of characters comes before us in these verses. In addition to those we have already met, Elisha and the King of Israel, we meet two women, an officer and four men suffering from leprosy. This unusual set of characters is gathered around the Word of God and two of its central themes: judgement and grace.

This passage is of vital importance for us because God's Word still sounds out the notes of God's judgement and his grace. Those who refuse to heed his grace will most certainly come under his judgement.

God's word of judgement (6:24-33)

After their confrontation with Elisha at Dothan, the Syrians stopped their raids for some time (6:23). After a while they seemed to forget the power of Israel's God and decided to try for a decisive victory against Israel by laying siege to Samaria. This strategy almost succeeded. Conditions became so bad that people were actually eating heads of donkeys, dove droppings and, yes, even their own children (6:24-29).

We might be inclined to explain the Syrian siege as something that just happened, but it was much more than that. Centuries earlier Moses had warned the people of Israel of certain calamities that would most surely follow disobedience to the commandments of God. One of these calamities was that foreign armies would lay siege to their cities (Deut. 28:53-57).

The people of Elisha's day had been anything but obedient to the Lord. They had flaunted his laws and had gone after idols, and now they were reaping the consequences. The God who is always faithful to his word had allowed the Syrians to surround Samaria. The Syrian presence there was, then, the message of God's judgement.

The self-reliant women

The citizens of Samaria responded to this situation in different ways. The two women of this passage quarrelled about a pact they had with each other, one which called for them to stave off starvation by eating their sons. Having joined in eating the first woman's son, the second woman was now unwilling to keep her side of the bargain (6:28-29).

Here we have a depiction of those who appear to be utterly oblivious to God's judgement and who with a self-reliant attitude resort to desperate measures just to sustain life upon this earth. How many occupy this camp! So taken up are they with the here and now, and the maintaining of it at all costs, that they never allow their thoughts to rise to God and the hereafter.

The defiant king

The king himself depicts for us yet another response to God's judgement. His was that of defiance.

The statement that he was wearing sackcloth under his royal robe might at first encourage us to believe that he carried a soft and tender heart towards God and a genuine sorrow for the idolatry of his nation. The author soon strips this hope from us. The king's pledge to behead the prophet Elisha shows that he was anything but repentant. He knew the city was under siege because Elisha's God had decreed it, and he would now show his defiance of God by killing the prophet.

The response of Israel's king, Jehoram, is also very much with us today. It is the response of all those who essentially hate God and take that hatred out on God's people. Let a preacher declare the holiness and justice of God against sinners and the certain calamity that awaits them if they do not repent, and the Jehorams of our day become angry. They may be content to ridicule him or merely to stay away from him. They may seek to have him fired. Or they may even threaten him with physical harm as the king did Elisha.

The messenger can only declare God's judgement. He certainly cannot change it. And those who ignore it as the women did, or defy it as the king did, will eventually find themselves facing it in its full force.

God's word of grace (7:1-20)

Judgement is not the only note that sounds in this passage. The grace of God is here as well.

This note of grace was sounded by the prophet Elisha to the king himself. The king, having dispatched someone to carry out his threat, followed along either to take pleasure in the execution of his order or, having thought better of it, to rescind it.

Elisha, knowing Jehoram was on his way, had the men with him bar the door against the executioner sent by the king. The king began blustering about the pointlessness of waiting any longer on God. God always seems irrelevant to those who have no place for him in their hearts. Elisha brought the blustering up short with a wonderful message of hope and grace. The Syrian-induced famine would abruptly end, and the very next day Samaria would enjoy an abundance (7:1).

In addition to short-circuiting his own execution, Elisha's message of grace set the stage for additional characters to enter the narrative.

The officer (7:2,17-20)

This man scoffed at the message of grace. No sooner was the promise of abundance out of Elisha's mouth than this man offered this pessimistic assessment: **'Look, if the Lord would make windows in heaven, could this thing be?'** (7:2).

A sour and shrivelled spirit that always makes us against everyone and everything is a great evil to be diligently avoided, but it is never more dangerous than when it manifests itself in rejection of the gospel of Christ. We have in that gospel a message of grace that makes Elisha's message of grace pale in comparison. The gospel comes to us in our spiritual poverty and tells us that God has provided spiritual abundance for all who believe. It tells us that God has, as it were, made windows in heaven. Through the redeeming work of his Son, Jesus Christ, God now pours out of those windows forgiveness of sins, adoption into his family, the hope of eternal glory and every spiritual blessing. But there are many who scoff at God's plan of salvation and refuse to accept it.

What a warning this officer is for all such! His rejection led to his ruin. Elisha responded to his rejection by assuring him that he would see the abundance but would not share in it (7:2). The prophet's word was fulfilled in the most frightful manner when this man was the very next day trampled to death

by the people who were in a frenzy to reach the abundance
(7:19-20). God's message of grace had become a message of
judgement for this hard-hearted, sour man, and God's message of grace in the gospel will finally turn to eternal judgement for all those who reject it.

The four men with leprosy (7:3-16)

Additional responses to Elisha's message of grace are reflected
by the four men suffering from leprosy. These men rejoiced in
it themselves and shared it with others.

These four men, on the brink of starvation, formulated a
last-ditch plan to save themselves. There was no food in the
city. There was no food in their lepers' camp. But there was
food in the Syrian camp. Perhaps the Syrians could be per-
suaded to be merciful and share their food with them. If not, a
quick death at their hands would be immensely better than
slow starvation.

So they were off to the Syrian lines. They were in for an
incredible surprise. We might say these men were surprised by
grace. God had caused the Syrians to hear **'the noise of a
great army'** (7:6). Thinking they were about to be attacked,
they fled. In their panic, they did not even take time to pack.
They left their tents, their horses, their clothing — and their
food! (7:7-8).

The lepers wasted no time enjoying the bounty. They ate
and drank and hid silver, gold and clothing. Then it occurred
to them that their city was starving. They said to one another,
**'We are not doing right. This is a day of good news, and
we remain silent'** (7:9). The four men soon shared their news,
the city was saved, and Elisha's word of grace was realized.

Christians cannot help but see themselves in these men suffering from leprosy. We too have been surprised by grace. We
were walking down life's pathway in our sin and condemnation

when the grace of God intervened, showed us the desperateness of our condition and pointed us to the Lord Jesus Christ as our sufficient Saviour. How we rejoice in the saving grace of God that rescued us from our sin and gave us spiritual abundance!

But we need to let these four men speak to us at another level. They realized they were not doing right by keeping their good news to themselves, and we do not do right if we do not share with others the good news of God's saving grace. Let us, then, adopt their words as our motto: '**... come, let us go, and tell...**' (7:9).

There would be a second siege of Samaria in 722 B.C., and on that occasion there would be no miraculous deliverance. Israel's sister kingdom, Judah, would also see her capital city, Jerusalem, besieged by the Babylonians in 586 B.C. There would be no deliverance for Jerusalem either. Because God did not deliver his people from their enemies on those occasions, the first readers of 2 Kings found themselves in captivity and far from home. They would have had no difficulty finding themselves in this account of Syria's siege. God had sent them prophet after prophet to declare his word of judgement, but they had, like the self-reliant women of Samaria, turned heedless ears to the message and gone about their lives. And many had, like the defiant king, hated and resisted the ones who dared to deliver God's message.

Now they had seen God's message of judgement fulfilled. How they must have regretted their refusal to heed that message! How very blessed they were to have there in captivity another message from God, the message of his grace that promised deliverance from their bondage and restoration to their homeland! They could read this account of God opening the windows of heaven to deliver Samaria from starvation and be encouraged to believe that he would do the same for them. They had spurned the message of God's judgement, and they could now, like the officer, spurn the message of God's grace or, like the four men with leprosy, receive it and rejoice in it.

As God speaks to us in his Word both of judgement and grace, we must decide whether we will be numbered among those who spurn the message or those who receive it gladly.

13.
Lessons from a saint and a villain

Please read 2 Kings 8:1-15

These verses contain two stories. The first deals with an individual we have met before, namely, the Shunammite woman whose son was raised from the dead by the prophet Elisha (4:8-37). The second introduces us to Hazael, the future King of Syria. The two episodes covered in these verses seem at first to be unrelated, but they are bound together by the larger story that dominates the first part of 2 Kings — the account of how the God of heaven used the prophet Elisha.

In the first, the King of Israel asks Gehazi to relate the great things Elisha had done (8:4). In the second, Elisha himself meets Hazael. Gehazi's presence in the first episode probably means that 2 Kings does not always present its accounts in chronological fashion. This episode would have occurred before Gehazi was stricken with leprosy.

These two narratives also have something else in common. They point beyond themselves to timeless spiritual truths.

The saintly Shunammite woman (8:1-6)

Elisha's regard for the Shunammite woman comes out very plainly in this passage. When the Lord revealed to him the approach of seven years of famine, Elisha urged the Shunammite to spend those years in another land (8:1). The woman did as Elisha suggested and spent the famine years in the land of the Philistines (8:2).

The famine was only one trouble for this woman. The fact that her husband is not mentioned in these verses indicates that he had died. And then there was the problem with her land. G. H. Jones writes, '... property left temporarily was taken over by the crown and was held in trust until reclaimed by the legal owner.'[1] When she finally returned to Israel, then, the first item of business facing this woman was seeking to have her land restored (8:3). Astonishingly enough, she undertook this appeal at precisely the moment when Gehazi was telling the king how Elisha had raised her son (8:5).

When the woman verified Gehazi's account of Elisha's raising her son, the king was so moved that he ordered an official to restore her land immediately, along with any proceeds that were received from it during her absence (8:6).

The captives in Babylon would have been profoundly encouraged by this episode to look forward to their own land being restored.

Confirmation of God's Word

The account of this woman speaks to us on a couple of levels. First, we can say that she stands as yet another reminder of the Word of God being confirmed and vindicated. In leaving the land during the famine, she had obeyed the prophet Elisha. By the king's action in returning her land plus the profit from it, she was given evidence that she had done the right thing in obeying Elisha. Those who obey the Word of God always do the right thing.

An example of the gospel

Secondly, this woman gives us a shining example of the gospel of Christ.

The gospel is not hard to spot in this account. This woman had a very serious problem solved simply because Gehazi related the good news about Elisha. And it should be noted that the account emphasizes the fact that Elisha had raised the woman's son from the dead (8:1,5). In like manner the gospel of Christ is good news about one who raised others from the dead and was himself raised — that is, Jesus Christ. As this good news is proclaimed, sinners are saved from the most serious of all problems, eternal condemnation.[2]

The fact that the good news about Christ has such power tells us that the church's central task is proclaiming it. Many these days argue that the church must become up to date. Their point is well taken as far as some matters are concerned. But in another sense, the church is called upon to live in the past. If she is true to her calling, she will focus on the good news about the Lord Jesus Christ leaving the glories of heaven, taking unto himself our humanity, living in perfect obedience to God's holy law, dying as the substitute for sinners and rising from the grave. This is the church's message. It is a life-changing message, and the church's task is not to modify it or update it, but rather to proclaim it faithfully all around.

The sharing of the good news about Elisha's deeds led to this woman's lost inheritance being restored. And the good news about Christ's mighty saving deeds leads to sinners receiving an eternal inheritance in heaven (1 Peter 1:3-4). By the way, as Raymond B. Dillard points out, once they have received that inheritance, it will never be lost by the children of God as they sojourn in this world.[3]

The villainous Hazael (8:7-15)

The second episode of our passage finds Elisha the prophet in Damascus of Syria. No explanation is given us for his presence. Perhaps he was there to at long last carry out the command given to his predecessor Elijah to anoint Hazael as king over Syria (1 Kings 19:15).

Ben-Hadad, who had ruled Syria for many years, was sick when Elisha arrived. Upon learning of the prophet's presence, he sent his officer Hazael to enquire whether he would recover from his illness. This reminds us of the opening chapter of 2 Kings. When Ahaziah, King of Israel, was injured, he sought help from Baal rather than the prophet Elijah. How ironic that the king of God's nation, Israel, should spurn the Lord's prophet while the king of a pagan nation would turn to him!

When Hazael arrived, with a lavish gift in tow, he put Ben-Hadad's question before Elisha: **'Shall I recover from this disease?'** (8:9). Elisha's answer is somewhat puzzling: **'Go, say to him, "You shall certainly recover." However the LORD has shown me that he will really die'** (8:10). Elisha was not trying to equivocate. He was essentially saying that Ben-Hadad would indeed recover if he were left alone, but he was not going to be left alone. Elisha knew that Hazael would assassinate Ben-Hadad.

Without actually revealing what he knew about Ben-Hadad's death, Elisha gazed upon Hazael with a prolonged stare and then began to weep (8:11). When Hazael asked why he was weeping, Elisha answered, **'Because I know the evil that you will do to the children of Israel: Their strongholds you will set on fire, and their young men you will kill with the sword; and you will dash their children, and rip open their women with child'** (8:12).

S. G. DeGraaf explains the prophet's weeping with this observation: 'Here the Lord was having an enemy of His people anointed! It was as if the Lord had forsaken His people and was on the side of their enemies. Apparently the Lord had changed into an enemy of His people. At the same time He loved them in the Christ. What grieved Him most was that He had to chastise them so severely. It was this divine sorrow that was revealed in Elisha's weeping.'[4] We see divine sorrow also when the Lord Jesus wept over the people of Jerusalem because they too would have to endure severe chastisement (Luke 19:41-44).

After hearing Elisha's explanation of why he was weeping, Hazael asked, **'But what is your servant — a dog, that he should do this gross thing?'** (8:13). The word 'dog' conveys insignificance or unimportance. Hazael was, in feigned humility, claiming that he was of such little account that he would never be able to accomplish such a great feat.

Elisha answered Hazael's protest by saying, **'The LORD has shown me that you will become king over Syria'** (8:13). The day after he returned from meeting Elisha, Hazael smothered Ben-Hadad (8:15). While the text does not explicitly say that Elisha anointed Hazael as king, it is very likely that he did so immediately after saying to Hazael, 'The LORD has shown me that you will become king over Syria' (8:13).

What are we to learn from Elisha's meeting with Hazael?

The faithfulness of God

In the first place, we see again the faithfulness of God to perform his purposes. It had been a long time since the Lord had commanded Elijah to anoint Hazael (1 Kings 19:15), a command Elijah can be said to have fulfilled in and through Elisha. But even though considerable time had passed since that command, God's will had been fulfilled. This teaches us not to interpret God's delays to mean that his promises have failed. The captives in Babylon must have eagerly seized on every emphasis on God faithfully keeping his promises. Their future rested squarely on that faithfulness.

The cost of rejecting the Word of God

In the second place, we see the terrible cost of refusing to heed the sure Word of God.

The people of Israel had been solemnly warned by God about the calamities that would befall them if they chased after idols. One of these calamities was defeat at the hands of their enemies (Deut. 28:14,25). The Israelites had spurned that clear word from God and had gone headlong after Baal. Furthermore, they had refused to heed the prophets of the Lord. They had refused to make a decisive break with their idols during the ministry of Elijah, and they had continued to refuse to do so during Elisha's ministry. God had been extremely patient with them, but now he was ready to hand them over to judgement.

The description of Elisha in Damascus is a startling and tragic thing. There the prophet anoints a foreign king! Here God declares war on his own people! And it was all because of their stubborn refusal to heed God's Word!

We are dealing here with a principle that has application for both believers and unbelievers. Believers are called to live in obedience to the Lord just as much as the Israelites of old. Those who fail to do so invite the Lord to bring chastisement into their lives. And the Lord can and will do this (Heb. 12:5-11).

Unbelievers are called to repent of their sins and trust in the finished work of the Lord Jesus for salvation. God has solemnly declared that all who spurn this message will suffer the calamity of eternal destruction. The passing of time may make that warning seem unlikely and implausible, but it will eventually be fulfilled.

14.
Walking Israel's way

Please read 2 Kings 8:16-29

For the first time in 2 Kings, the author gives attention to the kingdom of Judah. He does so by summarizing the reigns of Jehoram (or Joram) and Ahaziah, the son and grandson of Jehoshaphat. Because Israel also had kings with the same names, special care must be given to understanding which king and which kingdom is being discussed.

Tragically, Jehoram and Ahaziah shared more than just names with the kings of Israel. The author pointedly observes that they each walked in Israel's ways. He writes of Jehoram: **'And he walked in the way of the kings of Israel, just as the house of Ahab had done…'** (8:18). He proceeds to offer this summary of the life of Ahaziah: **'And he walked in the way of the house of Ahab…'** (8:27). Israel's way at this time was the worship of Baal, and Israel's way had become Judah's way.

We should not think there was no Baal-worship in Judah at all until Jehoram and Ahaziah came along. It is entirely possible that Baal had already made inroads into Judah in terms of the religious practices of individual citizens. We are to understand, however, that Jehoram and Ahaziah gave Baal-worship the official standing in Judah that it had long enjoyed in Israel. This amounted to a radical and sweeping change, and it certainly boded ill for the future. Sanctioned by the government, the worship of Baal was now poised to grow by leaps and bounds. We may rest assured that many in those days concluded that a particular practice was moral if it was approved by the government. How many these days believe abortion is moral for the same reason!

The beginning of the way (8:16-24)

Our author leaves us in no doubt about how Jehoram came to walk in Israel's way. It was largely due to the influence of his wife, Athaliah, the daughter of Ahab (8:18). This woman rivalled her mother Jezebel in devotion to Baal and in capacity for doing evil.

Under this evil tutelage, Jehoram excelled in wickedness. 2 Chronicles details his bloody execution of his brothers, whom he evidently regarded as rivals (2 Chr. 21:1-4). While the Chronicler does not specifically attribute this purge to the influence of his wife, it is very likely that she was largely responsible for it. The purge she herself would conduct with her ascent to the throne (11:1) is enough to convince us that her fingerprints were all over Jehoram's elimination of all possible rivals.

It was evidently during this evil time that the temple to Baal which is mentioned later was constructed in Jerusalem (11:18). How unspeakably sad and tragic! David's house, which had so often been a source of blessing for the people of Judah, had now become a curse.[1]

The continuation of the way (8:25-27)

The way of Israel did not die in Judah with Jehoram. It was continued by his son Ahaziah, and the reason is not hard to determine. His mother, the evil Athaliah, joined with other members of the house of Ahab to provide evil counsel to her son. The author of 2 Chronicles writes of the latter: 'Therefore he did evil in the sight of the LORD, like the house of Ahab; for they were his counsellors after the death of his father, to his destruction' (2 Chr. 22:4).

The best thing we can say about the reign of Ahaziah is that it was very brief, lasting only one year (8:26).

The end of the way (8:19-24,28-29)

In his summaries of the reigns of Jehoram and Ahaziah, the author of 2 Kings puts his finger on the trouble with sin, which is that it is always done **'in the sight of the LORD'** (8:18,27).

Every path leads somewhere. Jehoram and Ahaziah chose to walk in the way of Israel, and that path led them to God's judgement.

Judgement on Jehoram

God's judgement fell on Jehoram when Edom revolted against Judah. Jehoram mustered his army and marched against Edom only to find himself surrounded by the Edomites. By means of a surprise night-time attack, Jehoram was able to break out of the enemy's trap, but with his army in flight, he was unable to subdue the Edomites.

The Edomite revolt was only one factor in Jehoram's trouble. Libnah, a city of the Philistines, also revolted (8:22).

Judgement on Ahaziah

God's judgement also fell on Ahaziah. He decided to join King Jehoram of Israel in a campaign against Syria. This campaign resulted in Jehoram's being wounded. Ahaziah then went to Jezreel to visit the wounded Jehoram (8:28-29) and became, as we shall see, a victim of Jehu's revolution.

Judgement tempered with mercy

The author's brief accounts of the reigns of Jehoram and Ahaziah would present us with nothing but gloom were it not for this statement: **'Yet the LORD would not destroy Judah, for the sake of his servant David, as he promised him to give a lamp to him and his sons for ever'** (8:19).

The sins of Judah during this time made her worthy of destruction, but God, in keeping with his promise to David to give him an enduring house (2 Sam. 7:16) would not destroy Judah. David's line was not, of course, always visible — that is, there was not always a descendant of David sitting on the throne of Judah — but God kept the nation alive and God kept the line of David alive. And in the fulness of time God sent his Son to this earth as a descendant of David. Because Jesus was God in human flesh he, and his kingship, endures for ever. He is, therefore, the fulfilment of God's promise to perpetuate David's throne.

A warning

The reigns of Jehoram and Ahaziah provide a chilling reminder that ways lead somewhere. The way of Israel was the way of idolatry, and the way of idolatry was the way of judgement. The original readers of 2 Kings had walked in the way of idolatry, and they were now experiencing the judgement. They had arrived at the destination to which their way led. To change the figure, they were now reaping what they had sown (Gal. 6:7).

God's law of sowing and reaping is still in effect. If we want to change our reaping, we must change our sowing. If we want to avoid the heartache and ruin that sinful living produces, we must decisively break with the sinful living, saying with the psalmist:

I thought about my ways,
And turned my feet to your testimonies
(Ps. 119:59).

15.
Two abiding truths about God

Please read 2 Kings 9:1 – 10:11

After God created man in his image, someone has observed, man returned the favour. We have made a God with whom we are comfortable. We have done so by discarding the biblical testimony to those attributes that disturb us and by embracing those that appeal to us. The God with whom we are left is as tame as a kitten and as cuddly as a teddy bear. This is the era of the down-sized God. We now have a mini-version of God about whom we preach sermonettes.

The only problem is that the God of our construction is light years away from the true God, namely, the God of the Bible. Our dislike for this God in no way changes or diminishes him. He does not abandon certain attributes because the latest opinion poll shows them to be out of favour.

We come now to a passage that sets forth some of the divine attributes that are so often swept under the rug. The prophet Elisha no longer occupies centre stage as the author shifts his attention to the kings of Israel and Judah. But his primary focus is not on prophets or kings but on the God who controls human history. Elisha sends a prophet to anoint Jehu as king, an act that was of truly monumental significance. Jehu was God's instrument to bring judgement upon the idolatrous house of King Ahab.

These significant events show the faithfulness and sovereignty of God as well as his avenging nature.

A faithful and sovereign God

For one thing, they show us that our God is a faithful and sovereign God.

Those who know the Scriptures come to this particular passage with the awareness that several things have been 'left hanging'. God had commanded that Jehu was to be anointed as king over Israel, but that had not yet been done. God had declared that the house of Ahab would be destroyed just as the house of Jeroboam had been (1 Kings 21:21-22). And God had said with regard to Jezebel, that godless devotee of Baal and cold-blooded murderer of Naboth, that the dogs would eat her by the wall of Jezreel (1 Kings 21:1-23).

While all these things were hanging over them, evil had been flourishing in the nation of Israel and, as we noted in the previous chapter, Baal-worship now had a hold on the kingdom of Judah. These circumstances might very well have caused many to think God's purposes had been thwarted and his promises nullified. But we are always wrong to equate God's delays with defeat. What seems to us to be an inexplicable and unwarranted delay is to God nothing more than waiting for the perfect time.

When we come to this passage that perfect time has arrived. God's purposes have, as it were, been crawling along at a snail's pace, but the sluggish, slow pace suddenly gives way to swift action. The servant of Elisha anoints Jehu, who races towards the city of Jezreel where he will find both Joram, King of Israel, and Ahaziah, King of Judah.

Joram and Ahaziah (9:14-29)

These kings were united by more than one bond. In addition to their family ties (the mother of Ahaziah was the sister of Joram), they shared a religious tie in that they were both devoted to Baal. Ahaziah was in Jezreel to visit Joram, who was recovering from wounds he had received in battle against the Syrians (8:28-29; 9:15-16).

When Joram learned that a company was rapidly approaching the city, and thinking that there might be important news regarding the conflict with Syria (9:14), he sent in succession two horsemen to ask, **'Is it peace?'** (9:17-19). To each Jehu responded, **'What have you to do with peace? Turn around and follow me'** (9:18-19).

When Jehu was finally identified by his furious driving as the leader of this band, Joram and Ahaziah went out to meet him (9:21). The author is careful to note that the two kings met Jehu **'on the property of Naboth the Jezreelite'** (9:21). Joram repeated the question he had sent his messengers to ask: **'Is it peace, Jehu?'** (9:22). Jehu answered, **'What peace, as long as the harlotries of your mother Jezebel and her witchcraft are so many?'** (9:22). It was then that Joram and Ahaziah realized their lives were in danger, but it was too late. Joram was slain on the spot and Ahaziah was pursued and put to death (9:23-24,27).

Jehu himself would also prove to be unfaithful to God, but at this point he serves as an insightful theologian. Rebelling against God may for a while seem to bring peace, but in the end it brings only ruin. The prophet Isaiah makes this point with these words:

'There is no peace,'
Says my God, 'for the wicked'

(Isa. 57:21).

Jezebel (9:30-37)

From there Jehu proceeded through the gates of the city where the godless Jezebel looked with disdain upon him and said, **'Is it peace, Zimri, murderer of your master?'** (9:31). Zimri was the seven-day king of Israel who had taken the throne by assassinating his predecessor, Elah (1 Kings 16:8-19). In applying his name to Jehu, Jezebel was accusing him of treason and probably predicting that his reign would also be very brief.

Jehu responded to Jezebel's insult by commanding her servants to throw her down into the street, a command that they were more than happy to obey (9:32-33). After trampling Jezebel with their horses, Jehu and his men proceeded to a place to eat and drink. While there Jehu, almost as an afterthought, commanded some of his men to go and bury Jezebel (9:34). When the men returned, they found only her skull, feet and the palms of her hands. The scavenging dogs had eaten her just as Elijah promised (1 Kings 21:23-24), leaving only those parts that were too filthy even for them. In his sermon, 'Pay Day — Some Day', R. G. Lee says, 'God Almighty saw to it that the hungry dogs despised the brains that conceived the plot that took Naboth's life. God Almighty saw to it that the mangy lean dogs of the back alleys despised the hands that wrote the plot that took Naboth's life. God Almighty saw to it that the lousy dogs which ate carrion despised the feet that walked in Baal's courts and then in Naboth's vineyard.'[1]

The seventy sons of Ahab (10:1-11)

Having completed his cleansing of Jezreel, Jehu turned his attention to Samaria, where seventy sons of Ahab lived. He did so by addressing letters to the officials of the city in which he urged them to choose a king to lead them into battle (10:1-3). When they fearfully declined to do this, Jehu sent another letter demanding that they execute Ahab's sons and bring their heads to him in Jezreel (10:4-8).

Jehu received those heads with these words: **'Know now that nothing shall fall to the earth of the word of the Lord which the Lord spoke concerning the house of Ahab; for the Lord has done what he spoke by his servant Elijah'** (10:10). Jehu was once again acting as a good theologian! All would have been well with him had he continued to be one. All that God had said he would do regarding the house of Ahab had now been fulfilled, and God once again showed himself to be faithful and sovereign — faithful in that he was committed to keeping his promises and purposes, and sovereign in that he was fully able to do so.

Ours is also a time brimming with idolatry and wickedness. It is a time in which Christians are frequently ridiculed for believing the Bible and its promises. It is a time in which God himself often seems silent and distant. In such times God's people can do nothing better than read of similar times in the Bible and take courage from its reminders that God is faithful and sovereign. His promises will be fulfilled and his purposes will never be defeated. When it seems otherwise, the key word for us to keep in mind is 'seems'.

An avenging God

The events of this chapter also show us that our God is an avenging God. Elisha's servant anointed Jehu with these words: **'You shall strike down the house of Ahab your master, that I may avenge the blood of my servants the prophets, and the blood of all the servants of the Lord, at the hand of Jezebel'** (9:7). What does it mean when we say God is an avenging God? It means he sends judgement upon the wicked. It means he inflicts punishment for wrongs done. Many find this teaching to be terribly disconcerting, but the captives in Babylon would have had no trouble accepting it. They knew their captivity was the result of God's inflicting punishment on them for their wrong-doing.

Some take the Bible's teachings about the loving nature of God to mean that he is incapable of ordering the kind of carnage we have described in this portion of 2 Kings. They explain such passages as this by saying that God himself did not sanction the bloody doings of Jehu, and that the author of 2 Kings wrongly attributed these things to God.

Those who hold this view forget the following truths:

1. God is holy and righteous and has a deep hatred for sin.

2. Ahab and Jezebel were responsible for the murder of Naboth (1 Kings 21). They were also responsible for the slaughter of many other righteous people (1 Kings 19:10). It is safe to say that many more would have died if something had not been done about Ahab's descendants.

3. God had been very patient with the house of Ahab, giving its members every opportunity to repent of their sins and turn to him.

When we have trouble with a particular teaching of Scripture, it is often helpful to ask this question: 'What would we have if this doctrine did not exist?' Could we really desire to honour and serve God if he were capable of sitting in apathy and unconcern as Naboth was dragged outside the city of Jezreel and stoned? Could we respect God if he had sat idly by and said, 'It doesn't matter that they have murdered Naboth. My love for Ahab and Jezebel is such that I cannot bring myself to bring judgement upon them'?

Others suggest that God did indeed operate this way in the Old Testament, but that he has now abandoned such judgemental dealings, that Jesus came for the explicit purpose of changing God from being judgemental to being loving. They point to the cross of Christ and say that it is the supreme proof that God is no longer the avenging God of the Old Testament but is now loving and non-judgemental. Those who hold this view see only part of the truth about the cross. Yes, it does manifest the love of God. Let there be no doubt about that. But it also manifests the holiness of God. There on that cross, the avenging God who never changes was actually pouring out his wrath against sinners so that those sinners will never have to bear that wrath themselves. The New Testament itself clearly asserts that the God of the Old Testament is still the avenging God (Rom. 12:19; 2 Thess. 1:6-9; Heb. 10:30-31; Rev. 6:10; 16:4-7).

This avenging God has declared that all will eventually stand before him to give account of themselves (Rom. 14:12). What a solemn and frightening thought! Is there any way that we can have peace and confidence regarding our meeting with God? Yes, thank God, there is! The way is Jesus Christ. The truth of the matter is this: we shall all stand before God, either bearing our own sins, or with Jesus bearing our sins. If the former is true, we shall experience his wrath in all its fulness. If the latter is true, we shall find ourselves exempt from wrath and given entrance into heaven. The most urgent and pressing matter in this life is, therefore, to make sure that we have repented of our sins and that we have genuinely trusted the redeeming work of the Lord Jesus Christ.

16.
Doing the right thing
in the wrong way

Please read 2 Kings 10:12-36

King Jehu of Israel constitutes a significant theological dilemma for students of the Bible. On the one hand he is commended for eliminating the worship of Baal from the kingdom of Israel (10:28). But elsewhere in the Bible he is condemned for 'the bloodshed of Jezreel' (Hosea 1:4).

How do we explain this? We certainly cannot say, as so many do these days, that the Bible contradicts itself. If we believe the Bible to be given by God, as we most certainly should, we must believe that God is consistent.

Neither can we say that God wanted Jehu to eliminate Baal-worship without the shedding of any blood. God himself made it clear that Jehu would be his instrument of judgement on the house of Ahab and that his judgement would consist of Ahab's descendants being destroyed (1 Kings 19:17; 21:21-24). When Jehu was anointed to be king over Israel, he received this word of instruction from a prophet of the Lord: 'You shall strike down the house of Ahab your master, that I may avenge the blood of my servants the prophets, and the blood of all the servants of the LORD, at the hand of Jezebel. For the whole house of Ahab shall perish; and I will cut off from Ahab all the males in Israel, both bond and free' (9:7-8).

How, then, do we reconcile these seemingly conflicting realities? How could Jehu be commended and at the same time be condemned for shedding the blood of Ahab's family? The answer resides in Jehu himself. He was indeed God's instrument, and he did what the Lord wanted him to do, but he did so with an impure heart. Jehu serves as a much-needed reminder that it is indeed possible to do the right thing in the wrong way. It is even possible to serve the Lord in a sinful way. The Lord is not only interested in what we do, but also in how we do it.

What was wrong with the way Jehu went about eliminating Baal-worship from Israel? I suggest that there are four major answers to that question.

Jehu's undue delight

First, we must say that Jehu went about his work with undue delight and enjoyment (10:12-14).

Jehu began his purge by killing Joram, King of Israel, and Ahaziah, King of Judah and grandson of Ahab (9:14-29). He also killed Jezebel (9:30-37) and seventy sons of Ahab (10:1-11). But he carried his purge even further by killing a number of **'brothers of Ahaziah'** (10:13). It is likely that these men were not 'brothers' of Ahaziah in the physical sense. They were probably political and military leaders from Judah who had no actual blood connection with Ahaziah.

It would seem, therefore, that Jehu was eager to take the work of God's judgement further than was necessary. In doing this, he was unlike God. The Bible teaches that God is indeed a holy God, and, yes, an avenging God (9:7), but it also teaches that he is merciful. While God judges, he does not delight in judgement. This is the reason the King James Version refers to judgement as 'his strange act' (Isa. 28:21).

Those of us who know the Lord must maintain balance at this point. We cannot deny, as so many do, that God sends judgement, but neither may we delight ourselves in judgement.

Jehu's pride

In the second place, we can say that Jehu went about his purging of Baal-worship in a proud way (10:15-16).

This comes out quite clearly in his encounter with Jehonadab. As a descendant of Rechab, Jehonadab was part of a group that wanted Israel to return to traditional ways. They particularly desired to see Israel move away from farming to shepherding. Because Baal-worship put so much emphasis on agriculture, the Rechabites would have been firmly opposed to it and would have welcomed Jehu's revolution. By enlisting the support of Jehonadab, Jehu was showing that his revolution was broad-based and enjoyed popular support among the traditionalists in Israel.

The interesting thing is that Jehu enlisted the support of Jehonadab with these words: **'Come with me, and see my zeal for the Lord'** (10:16). We might say Jehu did his purging without the proper motivation. He should have done it out of concern for the honour of God's name, but he did it to build his own name. This reminds us of the ever-present danger of serving the Lord in a way that calls attention to, and promotes, ourselves.

Jehu's deceptiveness

In the third place, we can say that Jehu went about his work in the wrong way because he did it deceptively (10:18-28).

A large part of this tenth chapter of 2 Kings is taken up with a description of how Jehu posed as a sincere worshipper of Baal so that he could kill the true worshippers of Baal. While some argue that the end justifies the means — that is, we are even entitled to use evil measures if the end we seek is good — the truth is that it is never right to act in a way which is contrary to God's commandments.

Jehu's lack of devotion to the Lord

In the final place, we can say that Jehu went about his work in the wrong way because he did it from a heart that was not wholly devoted to the Lord (10:29-31).

As we read the account of Jehu and his purging of Baal-worship from the land, we find ourselves somewhat mystified. We know that he was God's instrument of judgement, and yet we become troubled and unsure about him. While Jehu is running up a sizeable body count, we find ourselves thinking that there is something about him that does not ring true. We finally have our answer when we come to these words: **'However Jehu did not turn away from the sins of Jeroboam the son of Nebat, who had made Israel sin, that is, from the golden calves that were at Bethel and Dan'** (10:29). A moment later we find these words: **'But Jehu took no heed to walk in the law of the Lord God of Israel with all his heart; for he did not depart from the sins of Jeroboam, who had made Israel sin'** (10:31).

Jehu is indeed an enigma. He could see clearly enough that it was wrong to worship the false god Baal, but he could not see that it was equally wrong to worship the true God by means of images. While he was quick to spot the failure of the house of Ahab to keep the first of the Ten Commandments ('You shall have no other gods before me' — Exod. 20:3), he was unable to see his own violation of the second ('You shall not make for yourself a carved image...' — Exod. 20:4).

So while Jehu congratulated himself on ridding Israel of Baal-worship, he went blindly forward in worshipping God through the golden calves established by Jeroboam. In so doing he brought his own house under the judgement of God (10:30).

Jehu and the nation of Israel

We might have expected Israel's slide towards judgement to have been halted by Jehu's revolution, but it was not. Jehu's attachment to idols meant that the slide continued. While the form of Israel's sin changed, the fact of it remained. Israel no longer worshipped Baal, but neither did the people worship the Lord God in the way he demanded.

We should not be surprised, therefore, that this tenth chapter of 2 Kings closes with an ominous note. Hazael, King of Syria, **'began to cut off parts of Israel'** (10:32). In the actions of Hazael, the Lord was sending his people warnings of the terrible judgement that lay ahead, but Israel refused to heed the gathering storm clouds of judgement and continued lurching towards destruction.

Jehu would eventually prove to be a microcosm of what Israel herself would become before she was carried away captive. She too would come to delight in violence, and the prophet Amos would say:

'For they do not know to do right,'
Says the LORD,
'Who store up violence and robbery in their palaces'
(Amos 3:10).

Israel would also become filled with pride, and the prophet Hosea would say:

> The pride of Israel testifies to his face;
> Therefore Israel and Ephraim stumble in their iniquity;
> Judah also stumbles with them
>
> (Hosea 5:5).

Deceptiveness would also be characteristic of Israel, and Hosea would liken her to a 'treacherous' or warped bow that does not shoot straight (Hosea 7:16).

Finally, Jehu's lack of devotion to the Lord would become so typical of the people of Israel that the Lord would say to them:

> ... your faithfulness is like a morning cloud,
> And like the early dew it goes away
>
> (Hosea 6:4).

The contrast between Jehu and Christ

The account of Jehu would make for very depressing and sombre reading if we could not lay it alongside Scripture's account of another king, the Lord Jesus Christ. Like Jehu, the Lord Jesus Christ came to do the work of God, but, unlike Jehu, he did it without sinful pride and deception and with a heart totally devoted to God.

The work of Jesus was to provide redemption for sinners by receiving in their stead the penalty for their sins. Because he did that work so perfectly, nothing now remains for sinners except to rest upon his redeeming work as their only hope for salvation.

Those who refuse to do so will find that this same Lord Jesus has yet another work to do, the work of judgement. When he finally dispenses judgement upon all unbelievers, no one will be able to accuse him of being like Jehu. His judgement will be just and fair, carried out from a heart of perfect devotion to God and out of the desire to honour him.

The choice before us is clear. We can either cast ourselves upon Christ's redeeming work in this life or have his judgement fall upon us in the life to come.

17.
Beginning again

Please read 2 Kings 11:1-21

This chapter constitutes a major shift in the book of 2 Kings. Prior to this the author has focused on the northern kingdom of Israel with only incidental references to the southern kingdom of Judah (chs. 1-10). This chapter begins the middle section of 2 Kings in which both kingdoms are discussed in alternating fashion (chs. 11-17). In the last few chapters of the book, Judah is the primary focus of attention (chs. 18-25).

The author of 2 Kings was not, of course, interested in history for history's sake. Rather he was concerned about the spiritual history of both kingdoms. He was interested in explaining to his readers how they, the covenant people of God, came to be in captivity. It was not an accident. They had violated God's covenant. Their political situation flowed out of their spiritual condition.

The spiritual history of the two kingdoms, Israel and Judah, was substantially different. From the time of the division at the end of Solomon's reign, Israel had been ruled by kings who were not descendants of David, kings who led the nation into idolatry. In all the years of its separate existence from Judah, Israel did not have a single good king. Judah, on the other hand, was ruled by kings who were descendants of David.

While some of these were very bad kings, their influence was offset by that of several good kings.

Another major difference between the two kingdoms is that Judah experienced true revival from time to time while Israel did not. The passage before us brings us to one such renewal. Jehoiada and his wife Jehosheba were the instruments God used to grant Judah this renewal.

Desperately evil times (11:1)

It is impossible to imagine a more desperate and vile state of affairs. Incredibly enough, Judah was at this time ruled by Queen Athaliah, the daughter of the exceedingly wicked King Ahab and Queen Jezebel of Israel. She was in Judah by virtue of a political marriage to Jehoram. How much damage has been done by unwise marriages!

The godless Athaliah seized the throne when her son Ahaziah was killed by Jehu (9:16,27-28). From the time of her arrival in Judah, Athaliah had worked to get Baal-worship established there. She was able to have some influence on her husband Jehoram (8:18), but when her son Ahaziah died she saw her golden opportunity. Knowing she would never be able to win the kingdom completely over to Baal as long as the people believed in the promise of a Messiah coming through the line of David, she set out to extinguish all of David's descendants — even though it meant killing her own flesh and blood!

Behind Athaliah's hatred of the worship of God and her attempt to liquidate the descendants of David was, of course, Satan himself. The Bible's first promise of the coming Messiah indicates that Satan would indeed seek to destroy the Messianic line (Gen. 3:15). He never came closer to succeeding than when Athaliah was on the throne. But he failed. What an important lesson we have here! God's promises will never fail even though it sometimes seems as if they will. God will always fulfil his promises and secure his cause.

Heroic actions (11:2-16)

Hiding Joash (11:2-3)

All seems to be unrelieved gloom when we read that Athaliah 'arose and destroyed all the royal heirs' (11:1). But that is not all we read. The very next verse begins: **'But Jehosheba ...'** (11:2).

What wonderful words! Satan seemed to be having a field day with Athaliah as his instrument. But the Lord also had his instruments. Jehosheba, the wife of Jehoiada (2 Chr. 22:11), spirited away little Joash (also called 'Jehoash' — 11:21, 12:1,2,4,7,18) and hid him from Athaliah. For six years she and Jehoiada hid and nurtured him while Athaliah conducted her reign of terror, and during this period Baal-worship flourished in the land.

Jehoiada and his wife could have taken a fatalistic view of the developments under Athaliah. They could have excused themselves from responsibility. They could have said something like this: 'If God wants to preserve the line of David, he can do it without our getting involved.' They firmly rejected this option. We might say Jehoiada and his wife understood this vital truth: when God determines to achieve a certain end, he also determines to use certain means, or instruments, to accomplish that end. Jehoiada and his wife were willing to be the Lord's instruments in this situation. For those six long years, they hid Joash, knowing as they did that they would all be put to death if their plan was detected.

We surely cannot read about this godly couple without asking if we are willing to be the Lord's instruments in this time. Are we willing to lay aside our own comfort in order to stand for God and to be used by him?

Claiming the throne (11:4-12)

Jehoiada finally determined that the time was right to claim the throne for Joash and show the nation of Judah that God's promise to the house of David was still intact.

It is noteworthy that Jehoiada claimed the throne for Joash in a planned and orderly way. Guards were strategically posted and carefully instructed (11:4-11), and Joash was crowned king (11:12). Some Christians seem to think that planning and orderliness exclude any possibility of the Spirit of God working. They believe the more Spirit-filled we are, the less methodical and orderly we shall be, but God is orderly in all that he does. We have to look no further than creation itself to see this truth.

It should not escape our notice that the young king was given 'the Testimony' (11:12) immediately after the crown was placed on his head. The 'Testimony' may have been the entire Law of God, or a portion of it, perhaps consisting of the Ten Commandments, the duties and obligations of the king (Deut. 17:14-20; 1 Sam. 10:17-25) and the covenant God made with David (2 Sam. 7:12-16).

Removing evil (11:13-16,18-20)

It was not enough for Joash to be crowned king. The evil Athaliah and her Baal-worship had to be removed. Jehoiada commanded that Athaliah be executed, a task which was quickly performed (11:15-16) to the great relief and joy of the people (11:20). The people themselves rose up to eliminate every vestige of Baal-worship from the land (11:18).

True revival always includes elimination of evil. Since we are not living in a theocracy as the people of Judah were, we are not to eliminate evil by executing evil people, but we can and must seek to eliminate evil from our own hearts and lives (James 4:7-10).

Making a covenant (11:17)

With Athaliah out of the way, Jehoiada led the nation to establish a covenant. The author puts it in this way: **'Then Jehoiada made a covenant between the LORD, the king, and the people, that they should be the LORD's people, and also between the king and the people'** (11:17).

This covenant consisted of two parts. The first part, between the Lord, the king and the people, was the renewal of the covenant that the Lord had established with Israel under Moses. In this covenant the people pledged themselves to be the Lord's people and to live according to his laws.[1]

The second part of Jehoiada's covenant was between the king and the people. C. F. Keil says the renewal of the covenant between the Lord and the people '… naturally led to the covenant between the king and the people, whereby the king bound himself to rule his people according to the law of the Lord, and the people vowed that they would be obedient and subject to the king as the ruler appointed by the Lord…'[2]

Jehoiada, then, led the people to embrace the truths that God had revealed to the nation when he gave them his law. He also led them to order their lives in accordance with that truth. Or, to put it another way, God used Jehoiada to bring both reformation and revival to the kingdom of Judah. Reformation is the recovery of God's truth and the reordering of one's life in accordance with it. Revival is the powerful working of God, which brings life through the truth, and so enables this to be done.

The church today sorely needs both reformation and revival. How very easy it is to be confused about these issues! It
is easy to speak about the need for revival without seeing the
need for reformation. It is easy to desire spiritual vitality in the
church apart from returning to the truth that produces such
vitality.

As long as the church is content to deny the central verities
of the Christian faith — the sovereignty and holiness of
Almighty God; the sinful depravity of man; the certainty of
coming judgement; atonement through Jesus Christ enduring
on the cross the wrath of God in the place of his people; salvation by grace through faith; the essential nature of holy living — she will not experience true spiritual vitality. She can,
of course, seek to produce that vitality apart from these doc-
trines, but a vitality manufactured by human wisdom will never
be owned by God and will only take the church further away
from the revival she so urgently needs. David Wells aptly notes:
'Christian faith is Christian only to the extent that it has been
constituted by the Word of God, the Word that God has made
powerful and effective in the reconstituting of sinful life.'[3]

A consoling truth

Jehoiada's leadership of Judah towards spiritual renewal gives
us the opportunity to consider a particularly consoling truth
about revival. The kingdom of Judah had strayed terribly when
Jehoiada and his wife took decisive action. Even though the
nation had gone into terrible spiritual deterioration, she could
be restored. The people had broken their covenant with the
Lord, but here the covenant is renewed. Here is revival's glori-
ously consoling truth: we can begin again! Failure is not final
with our God. He is the God of the second chance.

King David of Israel found it to be so. He went off into terrible sin, but found forgiveness with the Lord. The prophet Jonah also strayed from the Lord, but the Lord pursued him, restored him and used him. Simon Peter denied the Lord Jesus three times, but he also found renewal and restoration, even to the point where he was mightily used by God on the Day of Pentecost.

The whole nation of Judah would come to learn this same lesson. The reformation sparked by Jehoiada did not last, and the nation slipped back into sin. God eventually judged the nation by allowing the Babylonians to carry most of her citizens into captivity for seventy long years. That captivity would not be the final word for Judah. There her people experienced true spiritual renewal, and God graciously restored them to their land.

I have no more cheering and encouraging word than this — our God freely forgives and fully restores his people when they sin against him.

What is your situation? Have you, like Judah of old, violated your personal covenant with God? Have you strayed into sin? Have you failed to live up to the commitments that you have made? You can renew your covenant with the Lord! Come to him. Tell him all about it. Repent of your coldness and your straying. You will find that God is immense in mercy and that he is ever ready to forgive you, cleanse you and use you for his kingdom's sake.

18.
The history of Jehoash, King of Judah

Please read 2 Kings 12:1-21

The Bible presents many sad and tragic figures. Cain, Esau, Achan, Saul, Judas Iscariot, Ananias and Sapphira are some of the names that spring most readily to mind. Any such list must certainly include King Joash (also known as Jehoash) of the kingdom of Judah. Paul House notes: 'It is hard to imagine a sadder case of moral failure.'[1]

The tragedy of Jehoash is that of failing to finish well, or the tragedy of not staying faithful to the end. He was the man who lived two lives. The first life, while not perfect (12:3), was generally one of faithfulness to God. The second life was one of turning away from God.

The history of a reign (12:1-3)

King Jehoash came to the throne of Judah after the brief, evil reign of Athaliah. His long reign of forty years began when he was seven years old (11:21).

The author does not apply to Jehoash the same formula that he applied to his good predecessors and that he will go on to apply to the good kings among his successors — that is, he does not say that Jehoash did right in the sight of the Lord while not taking away the high places. Instead he says, **'Jehoash did what was right in the sight of the LORD all the days in which Jehoiada the high priest instructed him'** (12:2). Immediately we sense that something is very much wrong here, and we wait for the other shoe to drop.

While we wait we again celebrate the life of Jehoiada and the power of godly influence. What a man Jehoiada was! His greatness was such that the author of Chronicles tells us that he was buried among the kings in Jerusalem because 'he had done good in Israel, both toward God and his house' (2 Chr. 24:16). No one can desire a greater epitaph.

We are all in a position to exert a godly influence on others. Are we taking full advantage of that opportunity?

The history of a special achievement (12:4-16)

It was undoubtedly under the guidance and supervision of Jehoiada that Jehoash was led to call for the renovation of the temple, which had fallen into a most lamentable state during the reign of Athaliah.

The king's initial plan to restore the temple did not meet with success. He put the matter of raising the necessary funds in the hands of the priests. It called for the priests to set aside part of the normal temple revenue in addition to receiving special donations (12:4-5). The plan seemed sound and sensible but, for unspecified reasons, it did not work. The author simply says, **'Now it was so, by the twenty-third year of King Jehoash, that the priests had not repaired the damages of the temple'** (12:6).

Perhaps, as S. G. DeGraaf suggests, all the money that came in was diverted for the regular services of the temple which had been reinstated.[2] Whatever the cause of the failure, it was apparent that a new approach was needed. That approach consisted of a collection box set at the entrance to the temple

(12:9). This plan met with resounding success as the needed funds poured in. The money was distributed into the hands of the foremen, evidently in the form of 'block grants'[3] (12:11-12). No itemized accounting of their use of the money was required, **'for they dealt faithfully'** (12:15).

The renovation of the temple shows us the importance of persistence in doing the right thing. When his first plan failed, Jehoash refused to give up. It is so very easy for us to become discouraged in the work of the Lord. When things do not go as we hope, we often throw in the towel. Let us learn from Jehoash not to give up in spiritual endeavours. Keep praying. Keep attending the house of the Lord. Keep reading his Word. Persistence in these matters will finally yield rich benefits. Matthew Henry wisely says, 'Church work is usually slow work, but it is a pity that churchmen, of all men, should be slow at it.'[4]

The history of the end (12:17-21)

The author abruptly ends his description of Jehoash's successful renovation programme with these words: **'Hazael king of Syria went up and fought against Gath, and took it; then Hazael set his face to go up to Jerusalem'** (12:17).

Jehoash responded to this threat by giving to Hazael **'all the sacred things'** of the temple and the king's house. The result was that Hazael **'went away from Jerusalem'** (12:18). So Jehoash successfully bribed Hazael by plundering the temple and his own house. Instead of looking to the Lord as his mighty resource against Hazael, Jehoash relied on his own wisdom, and we realize that this is not the same king who led so decisively in the restoration of the temple.

Jehoash's reign came to a sad and tragic end when he died at the hands of his servants who had **'formed a conspiracy...'** (12:20).

The heart behind the history

The author's summary of the end of Jehoash's reign gives us the clear impression that something was terribly amiss with him during his last years. The author of 2 Chronicles identifies the problem in detailed fashion. It tells us that Jehoash turned from God in a most revolting fashion (2 Chr. 24:15-25).

This leaves us wondering why the author of 2 Kings did not give the details of Jehoash's apostasy. Some have suggested that his appreciation for Jehoash's accomplishments caused him to sanitize the record. It has even been suggested that he did not consider the king's apostasy to be moral failure but rather due to senility.

It appears more likely that the author chose to order his account of Jehoash in such a way that his renovation of the temple would stand out in stark relief against his later plundering of it. R. L. Hubbard makes this point: 'Once a promising, God-fearing young ruler, Joash died a disappointment. By bribing Hazael with Temple treasures, he tarnished his one great achievement, the Temple restoration.'[5]

The fact that Jehoash in his later years could plunder that which he had so vigorously promoted earlier in his reign suggests that the work of renovation never really came from his heart. With all his interest in the temple, Jehoash had failed to truly love the Lord to whom the temple was designed to point. It is easy to turn against the house of the Lord when we do not truly love the Lord of the house.

Jehoash's apostasy teaches us the terrible danger of letting devotion to the externals of religion blind us to our true spiritual condition. It was commendable for him to seek the repair of the house of the Lord, but he may very well have thought that by doing so he was truly devoted to God. Alexander Maclaren points out that it was much easier to get contributions for the temple than it was to kneel and pray. He writes, '... there is nothing that masks his own soul from a man more than setting him to do something for Christianity and God's Church, while in his inmost being he has not yielded himself to God.'[6]

The captives in Babylon certainly needed this point because they themselves had done the same as Jehoash. For many years prior to their captivity they had embraced only the externals of true religion. Jeremiah the prophet saw this and soundly rebuked them for professing to love the temple without being willing to amend their ways (Jer. 7:1-15).

The Lord Jesus himself confronted the Pharisees with doing the same:

Well did Isaiah prophesy of you hypocrites, as it is written:

'This people honours me with their lips,
But their heart is far from me'

(Mark 7:6).

The history of Jehoash is, therefore, the history of a man whose heart was never truly devoted to God. He stands as a lasting monument to the terrible possibility of being deceived about our spiritual condition, of having a faith in name only. What a fearful price he paid for his rebellion against God! This drives home the truth so pointedly stated by the apostle Paul: 'Do not be deceived, God is not mocked; for whatever a man sows, that he will also reap' (Gal. 6:7).

God's judgement is a fearful reality. Sometimes it begins in this life and follows evildoers into eternity. At other times the wicked seem to get away with evil in this life. But no one ever finally gets away with evil. The books will not be balanced in this life, but they will be balanced. God's holy and just character demands no less. Joseph Hall rightly notes: 'If ye have forgotten the kindness of Jehoiada, your unkindness to Jehoiada shall not be forgotten.'[7]

Each one of us is creating a spiritual history. Heaven is recording it all. If we are not watchful and careful, we can end up with a spiritual history much like that of Jehoash. We can start well only to finish in failure. It doesn't have to be that way. Our history can be entirely different. We can stay faithful to God all our years. If we fail to do so, we can heed the message of God's Word, repent of our straying and be restored to the Lord.

If we want the story of our lives to be a truly good spiritual history, we must look to the Lord Jesus Christ (Heb.12:2). He is our example. His spiritual history was one of such faithfulness and devotion to God that there was not so much as a single blemish or stain of unfaithfulness. We shall never be able to match our Lord's perfect record. Perfection for us awaits the life to come. But by diligently looking to him we can certainly see to it that our own personal history is a much better one than that of Jehoash. May God help us to be doing so.

19.
The tragedy of squandered opportunities

Please read 2 Kings 13:1-25

In this chapter the author shifts our attention away from the kingdom of Judah and focuses it once again on the kingdom of Israel. We cannot hope to understand 2 Kings if we do not always keep in mind which kingdom is being discussed at any given point. In these verses we meet two kings: Jehoahaz and Jehoash (or Joash). We shall be spared confusion if we remember that the two kingdoms of Judah and Israel sometimes had kings with the same names.

The two kings with whom we are now concerned continued the terrible legacy of the kingdom of Israel. While Judah had good kings from time to time, the kings of Israel were all of one kind. They were wicked men who disregarded the laws of God and gave themselves over to idolatry. It is no wonder that the kingdom of Israel collapsed long before that of Judah.

As we look at the reigns of these two kings, we must remember that our author was not interested in history for history's sake. This is history with a purpose. He wrote so that his readers could see the hand of God in history and so that they might deduce spiritual lessons and put them into practice.

What are the spiritual lessons taught by the two kings in this passage? I suggest that these kings show us the tragedy of squandered opportunity.

The opportunity to repent (13:1-9)

Jehoahaz, the son of Jehu, came to the throne of Israel upon his father's death (10:35). The author applies to his seventeen-year-reign the description that we have come to expect of any king of Israel: **'And he did evil in the sight of the LORD, and followed the sins of Jeroboam the son of Nebat, who had made Israel sin. He did not depart from them'** (13:2).

The matter to which the author gives particular notice is the way in which Jehoahaz squandered the opportunity to repent. We can only appreciate the enormity of this if we place it in the context of the patience of God, which was displayed in a couple of ways.

Oppression instead of obliteration

First, God chose to oppress Israel instead of obliterating her. From the time Israel broke away from the house of David and formed her own kingdom, she had been involved in blatant idolatry (1 Kings 12:25-33). God would have been completely justified in destroying the nation of Israel at any time during the years of her existence, but he chose to be patient with her. He was still showing that patience during the reign of Jehoahaz.

We should not take this to mean that God was ambivalent about the wickedness of Jehoahaz. He simply chose at this particular time a lesser form of judgement. He opted for oppression by the Syrians when he could have chosen obliteration. The author puts it in this way: **'Then the anger of the LORD was aroused against Israel, and he delivered them into the hand of Hazael king of Syria, and into the hand of Ben-Hadad the son of Hazael, all their days'** (13:3). The fact that the oppression itself was not an easy thing shows the seriousness with which God views sin.

An answered prayer

A second manifestation of God's patience was his answer to the prayer of Jehoahaz. There can be no doubt that this king was a godless man (13:2). We are surprised, therefore, to learn that he **'pleaded with the LORD'** (13:4). We are even more surprised to read that '**... the LORD listened to him**' (13:4). Other Scriptures indicate that the Lord does not, as a general rule, heed the prayers of the ungodly (Isa. 1:15; 59:2), but in this case he chose to do so.

How did the Lord answer the prayer of Jehoahaz? The account says that he **'gave Israel a deliverer'** (13:5). This deliverer is left unnamed. It is possible that it was Jehoash, the son of Jehoahaz, who, according to verse 25, defeated Syria three times and recaptured certain cities of Israel. But that would have occurred after the reign of Jehoahaz. The implication of the 'nevertheless' in verse 6 is that the deliverer arose, as a token of God's grace, during the time Jehoahaz was on the throne, but that Jehoahaz and the people continued in their sinful living.

Why did God show such patience with Israel? Why did he answer the prayer of Jehoahaz? It certainly was not because the nation, or the king, was worthy or deserving. It was rather because of God's own gracious nature. In particular, it was **'because of his covenant with Abraham, Isaac, and Jacob'** that the Lord refused at this time to destroy Israel or **'cast them from his presence'** (13:23).

The truly astonishing feature of this passage is Jehoahaz' response to the graciousness of God. It comes out with shocking force when we follow the sequence set forth in these verses:

1. 'He did evil in the sight of the LORD' (13:2).
2. 'Then the anger of the LORD was aroused against Israel' (13:3).

3. 'So Jehoahaz pleaded with the LORD, and the LORD listened to him' (13:4).

4. 'Then the LORD gave Israel a deliverer' (13:5).

We would expect this sequence to close with the statement that Jehoahaz and his people turned to God with all their hearts and faithfully served him the rest of their days. Instead we read, **'Nevertheless they did not depart from the sins of the house of Jeroboam, who had made Israel sin, but walked in them; and the wooden image also remained in Samaria'** (13:6).

This sequence is reminiscent of the recurring cycle in the book of Judges. There we find that the people of Israel would move into a state of rebellion against God. God would respond to their rebellion by causing one of their enemies to oppress them. The people would then cry out to God for deliverance, and God would raise up a judge to bring about the deliverance. But the Israelites, instead of devoting themselves wholly to the Lord, would slip right back into rebellion and the whole cycle would be repeated.

Many who marvel that Jehoahaz and his people should continue in sin after God had been gracious to them are guilty of doing the same thing. God's patience is designed to help us see our sins, come to our senses and repent, but we are inclined to take it to mean that we are getting away with sin.

The stubborn refusal of Jehoahaz to repent and to lead his nation to repentance only brought more difficulty. The King of Syria **'left of the army of Jehoahaz only fifty horsemen, ten chariots, and ten thousand foot soldiers...'** The author then adds this word of explanation: **'... for the king of Syria had destroyed them and made them like the dust at threshing'** (13:7).

The opportunity to do something great for God (13:10-25)

That brings us to the second of the kings in this passage, Jehoash, who became king after the death of his father (13:9-10). Jehoash was the second descendant of Jehu to rule.

The author gives very little attention to the sixteen-year-reign of this man. He simply notes that he also **'did evil in the sight of the LORD'** and that he **'did not depart from all the sins of Jeroboam the son of Nebat'** (13:11). But having given that general description of Jehoash's reign, the author proceeds to fasten our attention on one event — that is, his visit to Elisha when the prophet was dying (13:14-19). At this point Jehoash squandered the opportunity to achieve something great for God.

The poor example of Jehoash (13:10-19)

It is very instructive that the dying prophet still had the cause of God and the welfare of God's people on his mind. Having asked Jehoash to take a bow and some arrows (13:15), Elisha put his hand on the king's and told him to shoot an arrow eastward towards Syria (13:17). Then Elisha told the king to strike the ground with the arrows, that is, to shoot the rest of the arrows so they would strike the ground. With five or six remaining in the quiver, the king shot only three.

Elisha was enraged. He had designed a test for the king, and the king had failed it. Each arrow was intended by the prophet to represent a victory over Syria. The response of faith would have been to fire all the arrows, which would have meant the complete destruction of this cruel enemy of the people of God, but the three arrows fired by Jehoash would amount to only partial victory (13:18-20).

Some will argue that Elisha should have told the king in advance what he intended the arrows to signify. But Elisha had already said as much. When Jehoash shot the first arrow, the prophet said, **'The arrow of the LORD's deliverance and the arrow of deliverance from Syria; for you must strike the Syrians at Aphek till you have destroyed them'** (13:17). If the shooting of the one arrow represented military victory over Syria, why would Jehoash not assume that shooting the other arrows would represent the same?

Jehoash's problem was not that he did not understand what the prophet was driving at, but rather that he did not possess the desire and the will to win the complete victory. Alexander Maclaren rightly asks concerning Jehoash, 'If he had been roused and stirred by what had gone before; if he had any earnestness of belief in the power that was communicated, and any eagerness of desire to realize the promises that had been given of complete victory, what would he have done?'[1]

Elisha's prophecy proved true, and Jehoash was able to defeat the Syrians three times and to recapture cities that they had taken (13:22-25).

While we are certainly not free to count Jehoash as a true child of God (13:11), those who are children of God can certainly learn from him. There are several important parallels between this episode from ancient history and our own day.

Just as Israel at that time had real and dangerous enemies, so the people of God have powerful spiritual foes (Eph. 6:12). Just as Elisha symbolically conveyed the communication of his own spirit and power to the king by laying his hands on the king's hands, so God's people today are assured that they have the resources of heaven with them as they carry out their spiritual responsibilities.

But, alas, a further parallel is most sombre indeed: just as victory over the Syrians was negated by Jehoash's limited vision and feeble efforts, so many of us fail to realize great spiritual victories because of our own small desires, small interests, small expectations and lack of willingness to exert ourselves. God is free, of course, to work without us and even to work around us, but the reality is that he has chosen to work through us, and in some mysterious kind of way there is a sense in which God allows himself to be bound and limited by the unbelief, the apathy and the small desires of his very own people!

What we have seen makes it clear that while these may be ancient stories, they carry a very up-to-date message. The tragedy of squandered opportunity can become our tragedy. It will be the tragedy of all unbelievers who do not take advantage of God's patience and repent. It will also be the tragedy of believers who fail by their own limited vision to achieve great spiritual victories.

We would do well to heed these words from Ronald S. Wallace: 'The cure for all our shameful and self-centred half-heartedness in the Church today is possible if we realize that God never loses His enthusiasm for His Gospel and His cause. His fire never wanes. He never slackens or grows weary of His purposes. Because of this He is always ready to kindle our cold hearts with new warmth and vision.'[2]

The good example of Elisha (13:20-21)

Elisha's rebuke of Jehoash is the last of his recorded acts. Shortly after this he stepped off the stage of human history as one of the noblest men ever to occupy it. Elisha did not squander the opportunity given to him by God. He was called to stand for God and declare his truth in desperate and declining times. Elisha did what he was called to do. He was a man of the Word.

Something of the greatness of this man is conveyed to us in the account of what happened in connection with his bones. Some people were about to bury a man when Moabite raiders who had been invading the land suddenly appeared. In their haste to bury, they allowed the body to touch the bones of Elisha. The dead man immediately came to life (13:20-21).

We must not dismiss this account. It shows that the Word of God which Elisha had so faithfully borne was still mighty and powerful even though the prophet himself had died. What comfort there was here for the captives! They must often have thought their nation was as good as dead, but because of the powerful Word of God their nation would live again. This very truth would be strongly conveyed to Ezekiel who served as a prophet in Babylon during the captivity. Ezekiel was taken in a vision to a valley full of dry bones and asked if those bones could live. He was then commanded to prophesy to the bones, and as he did so, the bones came together and were covered with flesh. Ezekiel was told to prophesy once more, and this time the breath of life came into the corpses.

The Lord left no doubt about the meaning of the vision. He said to Ezekiel:

> Son of man, these bones are the whole house of Israel. They indeed say, 'Our bones are dry, our hope is lost, and we ourselves are cut off!' Therefore prophesy and say to them, 'Thus says the Lord GOD: "Behold, O my people. I will open your graves and cause you to come up from your graves, and bring you into the land of Israel. Then you shall know that I am the LORD, when I have opened your graves, O my people, and brought you up from your graves" ' (Ezek. 37:11-13).

Israel went into captivity because she wasted the same opportunities presented in this chapter. She failed to achieve great things for God by not living up to her high calling and, when she was confronted by the prophets with this failure, she refused to repent. But her failure was not the end of the story because of the graciousness and power of the Lord God.

20.
Amaziah and the peril of pride

Please read 2 Kings 14:1-22

In the middle portion of 2 Kings, the author continually alternates between the kings of Judah and Israel. As we have noted earlier, we must always keep in mind which nation is being discussed.

The verses we are considering in this chapter bring before us King Amaziah of Judah. Amaziah comes down the corridor of history as a tragic figure. The promise he exhibited at the beginning of his reign evaporated and he ended his life in shame and tragedy. The cause of this sad journey from promise to ruin was pride. Pride always wrecks promise.

Amaziah lingers before us, then, as a testimony to the peril of pride and to how intensely God hates pride. Amaziah's life confirms for us the truth of other scriptures. The author of Proverbs says, 'Pride goes before destruction, and a haughty spirit before a fall' (Prov. 16:18). The apostle Peter adds this word: 'God resists the proud, but gives grace to the humble' (1 Peter 5:5).

The early years (14:1-7)

A general summary (14:1-4)

The author begins his description of Amaziah's reign with his standard commendation for good kings: **'And he did what was right in the sight of the LORD'** (14:3). While Amaziah was generally devoted to the Lord in his early years, he was not perfect. The author notes this fact by adding the comment: **'However the high places were not taken away, and the people still sacrificed and burned incense on the high places'** (14:4). Amaziah, his son Azariah and his grandson Jotham would all be characterized by this pattern of general devotion to the Lord with the qualification that the high places were not removed (15:4,35).

These high places were mounds, or knolls, that were used for worship. God was, of course, displeased with the high places that were used for idol-worship. After the temple in Jerusalem was built, he was also displeased with the high places that were used for the worship of himself. The temple was designed to point to Christ. In worshipping God on the high places, the people were essentially looking away from Christ and engaging in self-willed worship.

Even the best of Judah's kings had been unwilling to address the issue of these high places. Asa removed some, probably those used for idol worship, but not all (1 Kings 15:14; 2 Chr. 14:5; 15:17). Jehoash evidently refused to deal with the matter at all (2 Kings 12:3), while Jehoshaphat probably only removed those that were used for idolatrous worship and not those where sacrifices were offered to the Lord (1 Kings 22:43; 2 Chr. 17:6; 20:33).[1]

God is sovereign in the area of worship. He has the authority to determine what is pleasing to him and what is not. But sinful men and women delight in being innovators in the area of worship. Ever eager to 'improve' worship and make it more appealing, they do not hesitate to remove elements which God has ordained in order to embrace those that cater to the worshipper's desire to be entertained and to feel good about himself.

A fair administration of justice (14:5-6)

After noting Amaziah's failure to deal with the high places, the author points us to an excellent example of the king's doing right, namely, the way in which he administered justice: **'Now it happened, as soon as the kingdom was established in his hand, that he executed his servants who had murdered his father the king. But the children of the murderers he did not execute, according to what is written in the Book of the Law of Moses, in which the LORD commanded, saying, "Fathers shall not be put to death for their children, nor shall children be put to death for their fathers; but a person shall be put to death for his own sin"'** (14:5-6).

The phrase 'as soon as the kingdom was established in his hand' suggests that there was a period of political instability in Judah after the assassination of Joash. Amaziah was able to survive this period and secure the kingdom for himself. When he accomplished this, he executed his father's assassins. He did this to administer justice to these men for their crime and to assure that they would pose no further threat. But he did not follow the practice that was so very common among the kings of that era and conduct a general purge. Instead he complied with the law of Moses that forbade executing children for the crimes of their fathers (Deut. 24:16). Since the law of Moses was given by God, we can say that in complying with it, Amaziah honoured the Word of God.

A striking military victory (14:7)

Amaziah is also remembered for his remarkable military victory over Edom, which had been out of Judah's hands since the reign of Jehoram (8:20-22). This battle was fought in the Valley of Salt, which was located south of the Dead Sea and was often the scene of battles. It resulted in Amaziah's army killing 10,000 Edomites and Amaziah capturing the city of Sela. Giving it a new name, Joktheel, was his way of declaring the completeness of his conquest.

The turning-point (14:8-11)

Amaziah's resounding victory over the Edomites represented God's blessing on his reign, but he regarded the victory as evidence of his own skill and abilities and began to think that he was invincible.

With proud recklessness he soon challenged Jehoash, King of Israel, to meet him in battle (14:8). Amaziah received a stern response from Jehoash himself who compared Amaziah's challenge to a spindly thistle challenging a stately cedar (14:9). He then predicted that he and his army would trample Amaziah and the army of Judah as a wild beast tramples a thistle. To prevent any possibility of misunderstanding, Jehoash closed his message in this way: **'You have indeed defeated Edom, and your heart has lifted you up. Glory in that, and stay at home; for why should you meddle with trouble so that you fall — you and Judah with you?'** (14:10).

We might think Jehoash's response would have been sufficient to cause Amaziah to have second thoughts, but he **'would not heed'** (14:11). The results were catastrophic. Judah met Israel at Beth Shemesh, about fifteen miles west of Jerusalem, and was soundly defeated (14:11-12). Amaziah himself was taken captive (14:13), and Jehoash, to add insult to injury, marched into Jerusalem, broke down a portion of its wall and took the valuable articles that were in the temple (14:13-14). Amaziah was probably not released until he agreed to hand over certain hostages and a large amount of treasure from his own house (14:14).

The pride of Amaziah was the pride of accomplishment. His victory over the Edomites so intoxicated him with his own greatness that he believed himself to be invincible and also to be exempt from God's commandment against idolatry. The pride of accomplishment is ever with us. It can make our heads swell up to the point where we think we are in a special class and that God's laws no longer apply to us.

The last years (14:15-21)

In this section the author employs his standard formula to summarize the reigns of Jehoash of Israel and Amaziah. He mentions the burial of these kings, names their successors and refers his readers to Chronicles for more information. But he also gives us more information about the tragic end of Amaziah: **'And they formed a conspiracy against him in Jerusalem, and he fled to Lachish; but they sent after him to Lachish and killed him there'** (14:19).

The last years of Amaziah are shrouded in mystery. It appears that much of his twenty-nine year reign was as co-regent with his son and successor, Azariah. This period of co-regency probably began when Amaziah was taken prisoner by Jehoash. That term of imprisonment, which may only have been very brief, gave the people of Judah the opportunity to install Azariah as king along with his father, which indicates that there was widespread dissatisfaction with Amaziah. Pride proved very costly to this man.

The pride of Judah

We can be sure that the author of 2 Kings did not underscore the pride of Amaziah without good reason. Amaziah's pride has to be emphasized because it carried immense significance for those to whom he wrote, the captives in Babylon. Amaziah's life, like those of other kings, served as a microcosm for the history of the nation of Judah before it was carried into captivity and, in so doing, provided an explanation for the captivity. The nation of Judah had also begun with devotion to God and with the blessings of God, but pride had set in. The people began so to pride themselves on their covenant relationship with God and on the temple that they came to regard themselves as invincible. They also took pride in their supposed enlightenment. They would not be provincial and behind the times! They would be like their neighbours, importing their gods and emulating their religious practices! God sent prophet after prophet to warn them and call them back, but they were too proud to listen, and now they were reaping the harvest, as Amaziah did before them. Amaziah also served, then, as a powerful call to the captives to break with their own pride and humble themselves before God.

Someone has observed that pride is a very strange disease in that it makes everyone sick except the person who has it. In time, however, pride will finally make even its bearer sick as well. The people of Judah could testify to that.

The humility of the Lord Jesus Christ

The reign of Amaziah must have made the captives long for a king who would not fall prey to pride. That king came; his name was Jesus. Pride was so foreign to him that he was willing to humble himself even to the point of dying on a Roman cross to give his people eternal life (Phil. 2:5-11).

21.
Two long reigns of prosperity and stability

Please read 2 Kings 14:23 – 15:7

We are here given short accounts of two long reigns. Jeroboam II reigned in Israel for a period of forty-one years, the longest of all the kings of Israel. Azariah reigned fifty-two years in Judah, which included periods of co-regency with his father and, later, with his son.

Jeroboam II and Azariah held something in common other than the length of time they were on the throne. Their respective kingdoms both enjoyed prosperity and stability during their reigns.

The reign of Jeroboam II in Israel (14:23-29)

Jeroboam II and the first Jeroboam (14:24)

We may find ourselves somewhat shocked that the reign of Jeroboam II was blessed with prosperity and stability. He was as much an idolater as all his predecessors. The fact that he chose the name Jeroboam as his crown name indicates that he most heartily endorsed the religion instituted by the first Jeroboam (1 Kings 12:25-33) and that he intended, not only to practise it, but to promote it vigorously.

It is no surprise, therefore, that the author of 2 Kings uses for Jeroboam II the same formula that he applied to practically all of Israel's kings: **'And he did evil in the sight of the LORD; he did not depart from all the sins of Jeroboam the son of Nebat, who had made Israel sin'** (14:24). The false religion of the first Jeroboam had long been in place by the time of Jeroboam II, but, as Matthew Henry puts it, '… a sin is never the less evil in God's sight, whatever it is in ours, for its being an ancient usage; and a frivolous plea it will be against doing good, that we have been accustomed to do evil.'[1]

Jeroboam II and the Lord (14:25-27)

The success of Jeroboam's reign is attributed by the author of 2 Kings to the Lord. We should not expect him to say differently. Scripture teaches that God is sovereign, and no one can succeed if God has not so ordered it. Jeroboam II restored to Israel territory that had been lost (14:25). And this success was ultimately due, not to Jeroboam's shrewd political and military ability, but rather to the fact that the Lord fulfilled the word **'which he had spoken through his servant Jonah the son of Amittai'** (14:25).

Matthew Henry suggests that this refers to a later period in Jonah's ministry than the failures documented in the book that bears his name (Jonah 1:1-17; 4:1-11) and concludes that failure need not be final for God's servants: 'Some that have been foolish and passionate, and have gone about their work very awkwardly at first, yet afterwards have proved useful and eminent. Men must not be thrown away for every fault.'[2]

After attributing to the Lord the success of Jeroboam II in restoring this territory, the author proceeds to offer this word of explanation: **'For the LORD saw that the affliction of Israel was very bitter; and whether bond or free, there was no helper for Israel. And the LORD did not say that he would**

blot out the name of Israel from under heaven; but he saved them by the hand of Jeroboam the son of Joash' (14:26-27).

This statement reveals the compassion and the patience of God. The Lord saw 'that the affliction of Israel was very bitter'; in other words, her spiritual condition was most terrible and she was ripe for his judgement. But out of compassion and pity for her, the Lord, who was not yet set on her destruction, decided to send her a helper. That helper was Jeroboam II. By giving Israel his long reign of prosperity, God was granting the nation an extended opportunity to repent and stave off his judgement. But, apparently taking their prosperity to mean that God was pleased with them, the king and the people blatantly carried on with their idolatry and forged for themselves the chains of captivity.

Details of the wickedness of Jeroboam's era can be found in the prophecies of Hosea and Amos. These men focused on the moral and spiritual decay that lay at the very heart of the nation. Hosea linked the idolatry of the Israelites with the behaviour of his own faithless wife, saying that the people of Israel were guilty of spiritual adultery just as his wife, Gomer, had been guilty of physical adultery (Hosea 1:2; 2:2-5; 3:1-5).

Amos warned Israel about being lulled to sleep by the prosperity of the times and pointed to the corruption, greed, oppression of the poor, religious formalism, idolatry, immorality and disdain for authority that were also flourishing (Amos 2:6,7; 4:4; 5:10-12,21). In other words, the prophet declared that their apparent stability and prosperity did not equal real stability and prosperity.

The Lord is ever slow to anger and abundant in mercy but, as Israel would find, there is a limit to his mercy, and those who push it beyond that limit will experience his judgement.

Jeroboam II and death (14:28-29)

The author of 2 Kings closes his account of Jeroboam II with a note about his further territorial acquisitions (14:28), his death (14:29) and the accession of his son Zechariah (14:29). Jeroboam II's long reign had come to an end, and with it ended Israel's opportunity for a reprieve. Jeroboam II left behind a kingdom that was outwardly healthy but rotten at the core. Israel would now accelerate towards judgement.

The reign of Azariah in Judah (15:1-7)

After a period of co-regency with his father, Azariah (also known as Uzziah — 2 Chr. 26:1-23; Isa. 6:1) became the sole monarch of Judah when his father Amaziah died at the hands of conspirators (14:19-21).

The author of 2 Kings gives us a thumbnail sketch of his reign that can be divided into a general description and a special note.

A general description (15:1-4)

After placing the beginning of Azariah's reign in its historical context (15:1-2), the author gives this general assessment of the king: **'And he did what was right in the sight of the Lord, according to all that his father Amaziah had done, except that the high places were not removed; the people still sacrificed and burned incense on the high places'** (15:3-4). Azariah, like several of Judah's kings, was a good king who failed to remove the altars on which people offered sacrifices to the Lord, something which, as we have seen, was not to be done after the temple in Jerusalem was completed.

A special note (15:5)

The one special feature of Azariah's reign is presented by the author in these words: '**Then the Lord struck the king, so that he was a leper until the day of his death; so he dwelt in an isolated house.**'

The account in 2 Chronicles tells us that the Lord struck the king with leprosy because he sought to usurp the role of the priests by burning incense on the altar of incense (2 Chr. 26:16). But the author of 2 Kings passes over the reason for the king's leprosy to mention only his isolation. During this period of isolation Azariah was apparently king in name only, with his son Jotham handling the affairs of the kingdom (15:5).

Fair days, stormy evenings

We cannot leave Azariah without considering how much he was like his father Amaziah and his grandfather Jehoash. These men are united in Scripture with an unhappy bond. They began well only to finish poorly. We might say they were men of fair days and stormy evenings.

Judah's fair day and stormy evening

These three kings provide, then, a miniature picture for the captives in Babylon of their own history. Like Azariah, Amaziah and Jehoash, the people of Judah had prospered in their early years only to end in ruin.

Christ's fair day and fair evening

Even though they were in captivity, the people of Judah could look forward in faith to the promises of God being fulfilled.

The greatest of those promises was, of course, the coming of the Messiah. That promise was fulfilled with the Lord Jesus. Unlike Azariah, Amaziah, Jehoash and the people of Judah, he was perfectly faithful. He began his ministry in perfect fidelity and devotion to God the Father, and he continued and concluded his ministry with the same. Because he never failed in faithfulness, God the Father raised him from the dead, and he lives today as Lord over all.

A perplexing mystery

If the author had been concerned only to give his readers history, these long reigns would have provided plenty of fodder for his mill. But he skims over the details. Why did he give such short accounts of such long reigns? What did he intend his readers to glean from his accounts?

The author may have intended that one phrase from each of his descriptions of these reigns should catch the eyes of his readers: '... but he saved them by the hand of Jeroboam' (14:27) and 'Then the LORD struck the king ...' (15:5). Jeroboam was a bad king whom the Lord used; Azariah was a good king whom the Lord struck. This strange anomaly carried a great deal of significance for the captives. They must have been perplexed to no small degree by their situation. They, the people of God, were stricken as was Azariah. The Babylonians on the other hand were, like Jeroboam II, wicked but used by God.

This reminds us that the Lord is sovereign in all things, and he uses all things to bring glory to his name. He did not condone the paganism of Babylon, but he did not hesitate to use wicked Babylon to discipline his people. On the other hand, the Lord loved his people, but he would not spare them from the discipline they needed any more than he would spare Azariah.

22.
Disintegration and decline in Israel

Please read 2 Kings 15:8-31

The long reign of Jeroboam II (14:23-29) suggests to us that God was giving Israel one last opportunity to repent. When that season passed everything changed. We now have the impression of a gathering storm. One king after another comes to the throne and the Assyrians gather strength. It is obvious that Israel is declining and disintegrating at an accelerated pace.

The reigns of five kings

These verses take us in rapid-fire succession through the reigns of five kings of Israel: Zechariah, Shallum, Menahem, Pekahiah and Pekah.

Zechariah (15:8-12)

Zechariah followed the forty-one-year reign of his father, Jeroboam II, with a reign of only six months. That would have been long enough for him to depart from the false religion of the first Jeroboam, but he refused to do so (15:9).

His assassination, which occurred **'in front of the people'** (15:10), was noteworthy because it brought to an end the dynasty of Jehu and fulfilled the Lord's promise that four generations of his descendants would succeed him (10:30). Those descendants consisted of Jehoahaz, Jehoash, Jeroboam II and Zechariah, who between them reigned for a total of ninety years.

Shallum (15:13-15)

After assassinating Zechariah, Shallum reigned for one month before he was assassinated by Menahem. Matthew Henry says of Shallum's reign and assassination: 'That dominion seldom lasts long which is founded in blood and falsehood. Menahem, either provoked by his crime or animated by his example, soon served him as he had served his master...'[1]

Menahem (15:16-22)

Menahem began his reign in a most detestable and vile way. He followed his assassination of Shallum by attacking Tiphsah, the site of which is uncertain. This attack may have been intended as retaliation against the inhabitants of this town for refusing to recognize him as king, or to destroy followers of Shallum who taken refuge there. As part of this attack, the bloodthirsty and cruel Menahem ordered all the pregnant women to be **'ripped open'** (15:16).

Menahem's ten-year reign was further characterized by devotion to 'the sins of Jeroboam the son of Nebat' (15:18) and by his tribute to the Assyrian king, Pul (Tiglath-Pileser). This tribute, which Menahem exacted from the wealthiest people of Israel (15:20), was payment for Assyria's help in consolidating Menahem's rule against the threat posed by Pekah, who was ruling in Israel east of the Jordan river.

Pekahiah (15:23-26)

After Menahem's death, his son Pekahiah reigned for two years. During his brief tenure he also followed the path of the cult established by Jeroboam (15:24). Pekahiah was assassinated by Pekah who, after years of opposing Menahem, finally gained sufficient strength to take this bold step.

Pekah (15:27-31)

Pekah reigned for a period of twenty years, which may include the time from which he rose to power east of the Jordan.[2] During his reign Assyrian domination increased to the point at which inhabitants of the northern part of the kingdom were taken captive. Pekah's reign ended when he was assassinated by Hoshea (15:30).

Spiritual truths

It is clear that our author does not give us a thumbnail sketch of all these reigns merely for the sake of history. He inserts certain phrases into his account that bid us to look beneath the surface to discern certain spiritual truths.

The ongoing wickedness of Israel's kings

Our author drives this point home by continually including one phrase: **'He did not depart from the sins of Jeroboam the son of Nebat, who had made Israel sin'** (15:9,18,24,28). This phrase occurs, with some variation, in the author's description of each one of these reigns with the exception of that of Shallum, which was so very brief (15:13-16).

This expression takes us back to the early days of the nation of Israel, to the time when the single kingdom over which David and Solomon had reigned was divided into two — Israel and Judah. Jeroboam, the son of Nebat, was given the kingdom of Israel, while the descendants of David continued to rule over Judah.

Jeroboam I began his reign over Israel with the glowing promise from God that his kingdom would flourish and he would have an enduring house if he would walk in obedience to God's commandments (1 Kings 11:37-38). Even though Jeroboam had witnessed the terrible havoc created by Solomon's idolatry, he stubbornly refused to be faithful to God. He launched his kingdom by setting up a whole new religion, with golden calves set up at Bethel and Dan (1 Kings 12:25-33).

While Baal-worship flourished for a long time in Israel, it never completely replaced the false religion of Jeroboam and when it was finally eliminated from Israel by Jehu, Jeroboam's calves were still left in place. King after king had the opportunity to break with the idolatry of Jeroboam, and king after king refused to do so.

2. The faithfulness of God to his Word

God's Word will always prove true. The author of 2 Kings makes this plain. As he relates the reigns of Israel's last kings, he tells us that Zechariah was assassinated by Shallum. At first glance, it appears that this is nothing more than just another historical note. But it was far more significant than that. Zechariah was a descendant of Jehu, the king who had put an end to Baal-worship before plunging into idolatry himself. Because of his idolatry, God pledged that he would bring an end to Jehu's house (10:29-31). Zechariah's death marked the fulfilment of that prophecy. The author of 2 Kings poignantly marks that fulfilment by simply saying, **'And so it was'** (15:12). He obviously wanted his readers to know that God is ruthlessly faithful in keeping his word.

Those captives for whom the author of 2 Kings originally wrote could see for themselves the very truths presented in this chapter. They had witnessed at first hand much of the wickedness of their nation. They now knew how patient God had been with them. And they also knew that they were in captivity because his patience had come to an end and had given way to judgement.

Are you inclined to dismiss all this as ancient history that has no meaning or application for us? Many are. But this is far more than ancient history. The author has in fact laid before us a spiritual principle that has been in operation from the beginning of human history. It may be stated in this way: those who continue long in sin and disregard God's calls to repentance will eventually experience his judgement.

What is your spiritual situation? How do you stand with God? Have you received his forgiveness for your sins by trusting the Lord Jesus Christ as your Saviour? Or have you rejected God's plan of salvation?

If you have rejected it up to this point, please realize how kind and patient God has been and continues to be. The very air you breathe is the kindness of God to you. Each breath you take is one more opportunity that he gives you to repent. The very fact that you have come into contact with this message is yet another expression of his kindness and patience. But hear this solemn word: the patience of God is exceedingly long, but there is an end to it.

A day will come in which God will no longer extend opportunities to repent. A day will come on which God will bring all unbelievers into judgement. The sky will be rolled back as a scroll. Every mountain and isle will be removed. And the ungodly, realizing the enormity of their rejection, will cry for the rocks and mountains to cover them. But there will be no escape, and the wicked will cry, 'The great day of his wrath has come, and who is able to stand?' (Rev. 6:14-17).

23.
Two kings of Judah

Please read 2 Kings 15:32 – 16:20

After describing the gathering storm over Israel during the brief reigns of five kings, the author turns our attention again to Judah. While Israel had an unbroken succession of evil kings, Judah was blessed with a number of good kings. Jotham was one of these.

But the story in Judah was not one of unmingled success. She also had evil kings who led her down the path of judgement. Ahaz was not the first evil ruler Judah had, but he was the first for a very long time (it had been 100 years since the wicked Athaliah had reigned over Judah). And his reign marked the beginning of an era in which Judah would have more evil kings than good (six of the former, two of the latter). This era was, of course, to end with the nation of Judah being destroyed and her citizens being deported to Babylon.

With the reigns of Jotham and his evil son Ahaz we come to a significant turning-point in the history of Judah. King Jotham was a delight, while his son Ahaz was a disaster. Ahaz was the bad son of a good father. Someone has observed that there are only two kinds of people — the saints and the 'ain'ts'. Jotham was a saint; his son was an 'ain't'.

The good reign of King Jotham (15:32-38)

The kingdoms of Israel and Judah sometimes had co-regents in which the son of the reigning king would begin to reign before his father died. This was undoubtedly established to give the son much-needed experience before assuming all the responsibility. A co-regency was even more necessary in the case of Jotham, whose father, Azariah, was stricken with leprosy eleven years before he died (15:5).

The author commends Jotham for emulating his father's goodness (15:34). Unfortunately, he also imitated his father's failure to deal with the high places (15:4,35). This blemish was offset by Jotham's attention to the temple: **'He built the Upper Gate of the house of the Lord'** (15:35).

Matthew Henry writes, 'Though the high places were not taken away, yet to draw people from them, and keep them close to God's holy place, he showed great respect to the temple, and built the higher gate which he went through to the temple. If magistrates cannot do all they would for the suppressing of vice and profaneness, let them do so much the more for the support and advancement of piety and virtue, and the bringing of them into reputation. If they cannot pull down the high places of sin, yet let them build and beautify the high gate of God's house.'[1]

As good as Jotham was, he was not able to carry his people to goodness with him. The Chronicler notes that 'The people acted corruptly' during his reign (2 Chr. 27:2). True religion is always a matter of the individual heart, and godly leadership, while immensely important, does not in and of itself guarantee the righteousness of the people. We do well to remember that while Christians are to be wise citizens who vote for candidates that stand for morality and decency, true religion will not come through the ballot box.

The disastrous reign of King Ahaz (16:1-20)

When Jotham died, his son Ahaz succeeded him. He was, as noted above, a disastrous king, so much so that he could be called 'King Disaster'. Or we might join Ronald S. Wallace in calling him 'The Judas of Judah'.[2] Ahaz was indeed a traitor to his country. He led her away from the God who had so blessed her and whose laws ensured her well-being.

We can divide the author's account of the terrible reign of Ahaz into two major parts.

1. A general assessment

The author of 2 Kings first gives us a general statement about the evil of Ahaz and then turns to more specific details.

The former consists of these words: **'He did not do what was right in the sight of the LORD his God, as his father David had done. But he walked in the way of the kings of Israel...'** (16:2-3). This statement is staggering. It tells us that Ahaz failed to live up to the standard set by his ancestor David, but instead followed the very evil example set by the kings of Israel. These were men who, casting away all regard for the law of God, lived in flagrant idolatry. Much of our success in life hinges on choosing the right role models. Ahaz made a terrible choice.

2. Some specific details

Idolatry *(16:3-4)*

Ahaz was an idolater of the first order. He **'sacrificed and burned incense on the high places, on the hills, and under every green tree'** (16:4). Nor was that all. He plunged so deeply into idolatry that he actually practised child sacrifice, making **'his son pass through the fire'** (16:3).

This was commonplace among the inhabitants of the land of Canaan before it was occupied by the people of God, and it was such an abomination in God's sight that he had driven the Canaanites out and had given the land to his people. Now Ahaz, the king of God's covenant people, was practising the very same thing. He evidently did so without the slightest regard to God's solemn warning to the Israelites not to imitate the sinful practices of the Canaanite nations. Repeating the sins of the Canaanites would cause his people to experience the judgement that fell on the Canaanites (Deut. 8:19-20).

Can you imagine what this practice involved? Can you imagine taking one of your children, binding him on an altar, cutting his throat with a knife and setting him on fire? We recoil at the very thought, and we are quick to denounce Ahaz as barbaric beyond description. We would never do such a thing! And yet we do! Each year over a million of the unborn are sacrificed to the god we call 'choice'. God took note of this outrage when Ahaz was practising it, and we may be sure that he is doing the same today.

Seeking help from other nations (16:5-9)

Ahaz added to his sin by seeking to form an alliance with Assyria. His attempt to do so was prompted by the actions of Rezin, King of Syria, and Pekah, King of Israel, who launched a combined military campaign against Judah (16:5-6). Some think these kings took this military action to force Ahaz to join them in an alliance against Assyria. Others think it was intended to depose Ahaz.

Ahaz responded to the attack of Rezin and Pekah by appealing to Tiglath-Pileser, King of Assyria: **'I am your servant and your son. Come up and save me from the hand of the king of Syria and from the hand of the king of Israel, who rise up against me'** (16:7).

Ahaz paid a fearfully high price for this alliance, stripping both the temple and his own house of their treasures and essentially making his nation a vassal state of the Assyrians (16:8). The alliance would seem to have worked, as Tiglath-Pileser conquered Syria (16:9), but such an alliance with a pagan nation was strictly forbidden by God. The Lord had called the people of Israel and Judah out of the nations to be his own special people and, through their walk with God, to be a blessing to other nations (Gen. 12:1-3; Exod. 19:3-6). Furthermore, they were to live in dependence upon God. He was to be their resource and their security. When the people of God entered into an alliance with pagan nations, they were repudiating all of this, and God was not pleased.

Ahaz should have realized that he had a far greater ally in God than he could ever have in Assyria. The Lord graciously reminded him of this through Isaiah the prophet: 'Therefore the Lord himself will give you a sign: Behold, the virgin shall conceive and bear a Son, and shall call his name Immanuel' (Isa. 7:14).

With these words the Lord was directing Ahaz to where his real hope lay. It was not in Assyria, but rather in the covenant that the Lord had made with Ahaz's forefathers. The centrepiece of that covenant was, of course, the coming Messiah. It was as if God were saying to Ahaz, 'The key to success for you and your kingdom is in breaking with your idols and looking again in faith to the covenant which I established with Abraham.'

Ahaz and the people of Judah had brought a severe crisis on themselves by their sinful living. How gracious it was of the Lord to intervene in that crisis and point them back to the covenant on which their nation was founded! And, as S. G. DeGraaf observes, 'How sure God's covenant is that this could be said in such a time!'[3]

God's covenant with Judah was indeed sure. He did send the Lord Jesus Christ just as he had promised. And if Ahaz had only possessed faith in that covenant, he would have realized yet another provision of it in his own time — namely, victory over his enemies. But not having faith in the covenant, Ahaz failed to receive the blessings of the covenant.

God's covenant of eternal salvation through the Lord Jesus is still in effect. It has not been abrogated or nullified. But we must look towards it in faith and rest upon it, making it the centre of our lives. If we refuse to do so, we invite upon ourselves the greatest of all disasters — eternal destruction.

Importing a pagan altar (16:10-16)

Ahaz added yet another sin to his already long list. After the Assyrians conquered the Syrians, Ahaz met Tiglath-Pileser, the Assyrian king, at Damascus, the capital of the now defeated Syrians. Matthew Henry explains the purpose of this meeting in this way: 'Ahaz went, to congratulate him on his success, to return him thanks for the kindness he had done him by this expedition, and, as his servant ... to receive his commands.'[4]

While in Damascus, Ahaz saw an altar that looked far more beautiful to him than the one back in Jerusalem. Having determined that he must have an altar exactly like the one in Damascus, **'King Ahaz sent to Urijah the priest the design of the altar and its pattern, according to all its workmanship'** (16:10).

Finding the new altar completed upon his return, Ahaz proceeded to offer a number of sacrifices on it (16:13). He also moved the bronze altar built by Solomon to 'an obscure corner in the north side of the court,'[5] saying to Urijah, **'... the bronze altar shall be for me to enquire by'** (16:15). By these words Ahaz was indicating, either that he would use the altar for seeking guidance — a purpose for which it was never intended — or that he would decide later what to do with it.

With his installation of this new altar Ahaz essentially became to Judah what the first Jeroboam had been to Israel — that is, one who deliberately set aside what God had revealed in order to follow his own ideas and desires. Believing his own wisdom was a sufficient basis for religion, he did not hesitate to abandon the old God and the old ways. Many today follow in the path of Ahaz. Very sure of their ability to make religion more appealing, palatable and relevant, they charge ahead with innovation after innovation in both doctrine and practice. They do so, it appears, without realizing that if the old God is the only true God, he cannot finally be set aside but will eventually show himself to be the true God and will bring us to ruin for rejecting him.

The fact that Urijah the priest so willingly complied with Ahaz's instructions to build a new altar comes as a sad reminder that even ministers are not immune from the desire to innovate in religion, but, to the ruin of their congregations, are often in the forefront of dismantling the very truth they are duty-bound to maintain.

Abusing sacred articles (16:17-18)

The author adds yet another detail to the résumé of Ahaz's wickedness: **'And King Ahaz cut off the panels of the carts, and removed the lavers from them; and he took down the Sea from the bronze oxen that were under it, and put it on a pavement of stones'** (16:17). The author gives no reason for his mutilation of these temple furnishings, described in 1 Kings 7:23-39, but it seems likely, as C. F. Keil suggests, that Ahaz was either attempting to hide these materials in view of a forthcoming visit from Tiglath-Pileser, or else using them to decorate his own palace.[6]

Ahaz also removed **'the Sabbath pavilion'** and **'the king's outer entrance'** (16:18). The former may have been a covered stand in the temple court for the king and his attendants to use on special days. The latter was the king's private entrance into the temple (1 Kings 10:5). These were removed **'on account of the king of Assyria'** (16:18). This word of explanation gives the impression that, while the pavilion and entrance were not among the sacred articles of the temple and Ahaz was therefore free to remove them, his doing so nevertheless marked a low point in the history of Judah because it indicated his deference to Tiglath-Pileser.

What can we learn from these two kings?

What impression did the accounts of Jotham and Ahaz have on the first readers of 2 Kings? We cannot help but think they must have considered the lives of these kings to represent in miniature the story of their whole nation. Perhaps they looked at these successive accounts and shook their heads with wonderment and regret that their nation could so quickly go from a Jotham to an Ahaz. Perhaps they saw in Ahaz an illustration of their nation's pathway to ruin. Like Ahaz, their nation had gone after idols, vainly trusted in political alliances, imported false religion and abused the sacred. As they looked upon this account in their captivity, they did not have to wonder about the reason why they were there.

We are wise if we take the time to learn the lessons Ahaz teaches. We can, as he did, turn our lives into ruin and disaster by living in sin and refusing to repent. But we do not have to travel the path of Ahaz.

24.
The death of a kingdom

Please read 2 Kings 17:1-23

These sad verses report the death of the nation of Israel. The author functions here as a coroner. He conducts an autopsy on the lifeless body of Israel and hands down his official ruling. Israel's death was due to suicide. She did not have to die. She died because she chose to die. Israel did not die because of the Assyrians who invaded her land and carried her citizens into captivity. She was already dead before they arrived. They were merely the pall-bearers who carried the body away.

The author encapsulates the death of Israel in these words: **'Now the king of Assyria went throughout all the land, and went up to Samaria and besieged it for three years. In the ninth year of Hoshea, the king of Assyria took Samaria and carried Israel away to Assyria...'** (17:5-6).

The time of death (17:1-4)

These verses place the death of Israel during the reign of Hoshea, who came to the throne after assassinating Pekah (15:30). The nation was by this time in such a very weakened and feeble condition that it is surprising that Hoshea or anyone else should desire it. Matthew Henry says of Hoshea,

'Surely he was fond of a crown indeed who, at this time, would run such a hazard as a traitor did; for the crown of Israel, now that it had lost the choicest of its flowers and jewels, was lined more than ever with thorns, had of late been fatal to all the heads that had worn it, was forfeited to divine justice, and now ready to be laid in the dust — a crown which a wise man would not have taken up in the street, yet Hoshea not only ventured *upon* it but ventured *for* it, and it cost him dear'[1] (italics are his).

The author gives Hoshea credit for not being as bad as his predecessors (17:2), but he still did **'evil in the sight of the Lord'** (17:2). At this point Israel so reeked with badness that it could not be helped by a little goodness.

Hoshea was never king in the full sense of the word. It is likely that he came to the throne as a vassal of the Assyrians and continued in this relationship until he decided to withhold the tribute money from Assyria and form an alliance with Egypt (17:4). This fatal miscalculation caused Shalmaneser, the successor of Tiglath-Pileser, to imprison Hoshea and lay siege to the city of Samaria (17:4).

The causes of death

As we look at this author's account of the death of Israel, we are able to isolate three major reasons for it. We do well to study these because they are still at work, destroying nations, churches and individuals.

1. Disobedience to God's laws (17:7-12,16-17)

The author gives us a very long and depressing list of Israel's sins against God:

1. They feared other gods (17:7).
2. They followed the evil practices of the nations God had cast out of Canaan (17:8,11).
3. They followed the evil innovations of their own kings (17:8).
4. They tried to keep their idolatry hidden from the Lord by combining it with his worship (17:9).
5. They erected high places in all their cities (17:9).
6. They made use of sexually suggestive images (17:10).
7. They practised the abomination of child sacrifice (17:17).
8. They practised witchcraft and sorcery (17:17).

A mere glance at this list is sufficient to see that Israel's primary sin was idolatry. She gave to idols the devotion and service that belonged to God alone.

God had been very good to Israel, and yet she went after idols! The Lord had established a special covenant relationship with Israel (17:15). He had delivered the Israelites from bondage in the land of Egypt (17:7). He had cast heathen nations out of the land of Canaan and given it to them (17:8). He had given them his law to make them different from the other nations and to guide them (17:15). But Israel's kings and her people, with reckless disregard for God's commandments and their own well-being, plunged headlong into the worship of idols. And by their idolatry, they essentially said to God, 'You have not been good to us!'

Idolatry has not died. We may not fall down and worship crude images carved out of stone and wood, but we can still be idolaters. Every time we give to something else the allegiance that belongs to God, we are guilty of idolatry. We turn our backs on all the blessings God has bestowed upon us and accuse him of not being good to us.

How could Israel, with all her blessings, turn to idols? The answer is not hard to find. Her people wanted to be like the other nations. This evil propensity had been ingrained in Israel for a very long time. It was there in Samuel's time when the people demanded a king so they could be like the other nations (1 Sam. 8:4-5,19-20). It was certainly present when Solomon was king over both Israel and Judah. The fact that he married wives from other nations and worshipped their gods indicates that he was too easily impressed with the religious practices of these nations (1 Kings 11:1-8).

Just as the threat of idolatry is still with us, so is this desire to be like the world. The truth is that some of God's people seem terrified at the very thought of being considered out of step with, or behind, the times. They hear about evolution and try to synchronize it with the Bible's account of creation. They hear about the latest beliefs in the area of sexual morality and immediately try to water down the Bible's teaching to bring it into line with those beliefs. All along they fail to realize that the very things they are trying to synthesize with Christianity were born out of hostility towards it.

We come across a gravestone in this seventeenth chapter of 2 Kings. This stone marks Israel's grave, but it also stands as a lasting monument to the ability of idolatry, born out of infatuation with the world, to kill. Let us ever take heed.

2. Refusal to heed God's Word (17:13-14)

God would have been justified in sending judgement upon Israel as soon as she began practising disobedience. But in tender grace and mercy he refused to do so. Instead he sent prophet after prophet to warn the people about their sin of idolatry and the destruction it would inevitably bring.

These prophets also sounded a glorious note of comfort and hope. If the Israelites would only repent of their sins and return to the Lord, he would wholeheartedly forgive and restore them.

Hosea was one of these prophets. Hear him as he pleads with Israel:

> O Israel, return to the LORD your God,
> For you have stumbled because of your iniquity;
> Take words with you,
> And return to the LORD.
> Say to him,
> 'Take away all iniquity;
> Receive us graciously,
> For we will offer the sacrifices of our lips...'
> 'I will heal their backsliding,
> I will love them freely,
> For my anger has turned away from him,
> I will be like the dew to Israel;
> He shall grow like the lily,
> And lengthen his roots like Lebanon'
>
> (Hosea 14:1-2,4-5).

How gracious God was to repeatedly call the Israelites to repentance! But, alas, they refused to heed! Our author pointedly says, **'Nevertheless they would not hear, but stiffened their necks, like the necks of their fathers, who did not believe in the LORD their God'** (17:14). To be stiff-necked is to be stubborn or obstinate. It is to be, in the words of John Gill, 'unruly, like an heifer unaccustomed to the yoke, that draws back from it, and wriggles its neck out of it'.[2] The people of Israel were to submit gladly to God's yoke — that is, to the commandments which he had given them — but, like their fathers under Moses, the generations covered by 2 Kings had stubbornly refused (Deut. 9:6,13; 10:16).

No one ever experiences the calamity of God's judgement without obstinately rebelling against the Word of God that so plainly warns about it.

3. The faithfulness of God to his own word (17:23)

The third reason for Israel's death may come as something of a surprise. The author states this emphatically. He says, **'The LORD removed Israel out of his sight, as he had said by all his servants the prophets'** (17:23). Israel was judged because God had declared that he would judge her!

Long before he sent the prophets, the Lord had warned Israel about idolatry. In the book of Deuteronomy, the Lord repeatedly deals with this issue. Here is one example: 'Take heed to yourselves, lest your heart be deceived, and you turn aside and serve other gods and worship them' (Deut. 11:16). The Lord also specifically stated in Deuteronomy that idolatry would lead to captivity (Deut. 28:41,63-64).

When the people of Israel steadfastly refused to heed the warnings both of Deuteronomy and of the prophets, the Lord did exactly as he had said he would do. The Assyrians came in, devastated the land and took Israel's citizens captive (17:5-6). The Lord describes this captivity as his way of removing Israel 'out of his sight' (17:23). In this way God powerfully conveyed the gravity and enormity of his judgement. He is, of course, the all-seeing God. Nothing is hidden from his eyes (2 Chr. 16:9; Job 28:24; 31:4; 34:21; Prov. 5:21; 15:3). God was not saying, then, that Israel would be outside the realm of his knowledge or awareness, that he would suddenly become limited in knowledge. Rather he was saying that he would not be looking approvingly upon Israel, or smiling upon her. She was to be removed from God's favourable sight.

Captivity was a most fitting judgement. Israel had followed the ways of the heathen nations that God had used her to drive out of Canaan. And now God uses a heathen nation to drive Israel herself out of the land. Through this judgement, God essentially said to Israel, 'You cannot be partially like the heathen nations. You must be totally like them. If you insist on sharing their sins, you must also experience their judgement' (see Lev. 18:26-28).

There was another reason why it was very fitting that the Lord should use captivity to judge Israel: Israel had become a willing captive of sin; so it was appropriate that her judgement should come in that same form.

God, in his Word, promises good for those who obey him as well as warning of calamity for those who refuse to obey. The same faithfulness of God that brought disaster upon Israel for her sin was now a comfort to the readers of 2 Kings. They were those who were experiencing that captivity, but they had this promise from God: 'Now it shall come to pass, when all these things come upon you, the blessing and the curse which I have set before you, and you call them to mind among all the nations where the LORD your God drives you, and you return to the LORD your God and obey his voice, according to all that I command you today, you and your children, with all your heart and with all your soul, that the LORD your God will bring you back from captivity, and have compassion on you, and gather you again from all the nations where the LORD your God has scattered you' (Deut. 30:1-3). What a wonderful promise this was for these captives! The God who had been faithful to his word in bringing judgement could be counted on to be faithful to his promise to restore.

This faithful God speaks to us today. He promises eternal salvation through the redeeming work of his Son, Jesus Christ. But he also firmly pronounces eternal destruction on those who refuse Christ. If we will come to Christ, we may be assured that God will honour his promise to forgive us. If we refuse to come, we may be sure that he will honour his commitment to judge us. The faithfulness of God will be either a comfort to us or a terror to us. It all depends on whether we obey his Word.

25.
Mistakes in religion

Please read 2 Kings 17:24-41

Mistakes are part of life. We can't live without making them. Some are not serious. If we cannot name the capital of a country in South America, no real harm is done unless we are on *Who Wants to be a Millionaire?* Other mistakes, however, are very serious indeed. If a doctor makes a mistake, it may very well cost someone his life.

We live in a day in which it is commonly thought that it is impossible to be mistaken in religion. While readily admitting that we can be wrong in every other area of life, many people assume all religious views and beliefs to be equally valid. The Bible is against those who hold this notion. It constantly warns us about false teachers and their teachings. It continually says to us, 'Do not be deceived.' It tells us that Satan is ever busy to distort the truth. It records several instances of individuals who came to ruin because of mistaken notions about religion.

The verses before us stand as one example of erroneous ideas about religion. They enable us to identify three major religious mistakes.

1. Compartmentalizing God (17:24-26)

Here we meet some new faces. Several years after carrying most of the citizens of Israel into captivity, the King of Assyria decided to repopulate the land with people he had taken captive from other nations. When these newcomers arrived in the land, they found a small remnant of Israelites there. It was not long before the new settlers began to intermarry with those Israelites. Their offspring became known as Samaritans. When the Jews returned from their captivity, they immediately felt hostility towards this mixed race, a hostility that still existed during Jesus' ministry (John 4:9).

The new settlers had not been in the land of Israel long before they realized that it posed very serious challenges, one of which was an abundance of lions. After some of their number became lunch for the lions, these new inhabitants came to the conclusion that it was **'the God of the land'** who was responsible for sending these lions.

This was typical reasoning for these people. They were idolaters who were accustomed to thinking in terms of local deities. Each area had its own god, and if someone wanted to live successfully in that area, he had to learn about the god of the place and how to appease him. Each god had, as it were, his own compartment, and as no one god could possibly be sovereign over all, success in life hinged on worshipping many gods. These benighted people completely failed to understand that in worshipping many gods, they could give no real worship to any.

We might find this somewhat amusing, but we can do the same thing. We can construct a Sunday compartment for God. We can go to his house and seem to give him worship, and then live the rest of the week without even thinking of him, or seeking to govern our lives according to his laws.

Compartmentalism has become a very important aspect of American society. We constantly hear these days that evangelical, Bible-believing Christians who hold public office must keep their religion out of their decision-making, as if a person can separate everything that makes him what he is from his decisions and actions! In America the principle of separation of church and state has been turned on its head. The original intent of this clause was to keep the state from interfering with the church, but it is now interpreted to mean that Christian people have no right to exert their influence in government. Someone has observed that modern-day Americans are attempting to put God on a reservation, as the US government did with the Indians many years ago. We may think we are getting away with this, but in due time God will show himself to be what he has been all along — Lord over all. And those who think otherwise will cry for the rocks to fall on them when God finally reveals his sovereignty (Rev. 6:15-17).

2. Accepting religious authority at face value (17:27-28)

After having convinced themselves that God was a local deity who was responsible for the calamities that befell them, these settlers asked the King of Assyria to send someone who was versed in the ways of this god (17:26). The King of Assyria, not knowing the first thing about matters pertaining to the true God, complied with their request by sending them one of the priests of Israel (17:28).

This in itself should immediately cause us to smell a rat. Because the nation of Israel had no true priests of the Lord, this priest had to be one from Bethel, that is, one of the priests of the false religion instituted by Jeroboam (1 Kings 12:25-33). This religion supposedly worshipped the true God of Israel but used golden calves for doing so, a practice which God hated.

The settlers received from Assyria, then, a priest who was supposed to teach them the ways of the Lord, ways he himself did not in fact know. Yes, this priest taught these settlers **'how they should fear the LORD'** (17:28). But subsequent information makes it clear that he did not teach them how to genuinely and truly reverence God. The 'fear' he taught was only some of the outward forms of true religion. The apostle Paul shows us that it is possible to have the outward form without the inner reality (2 Tim. 3:5). These settlers received erroneous teaching from someone in a position of authority who was himself mistaken in his beliefs.

Satan knows far better than we do that authority is absolutely crucial in religion, that there can in fact be no true religion without it. People must know what to believe and why to believe it! Satan spares no effort, therefore, in this area. Knowing that Scripture is the true authority for understanding the ways of God, he constantly seeks to undermine it. He alleges through his various instruments that it is not really the Word of God. He suggests that there are errors in it which render it untrustworthy. He suggests that it is inspired only in parts and that we are inspired to pick out those passages and discard the rest. He argues that no intelligent, well-educated person believes it. There is no end to his attacks on Scripture, and once he undermines confidence in it, nothing is left except for each of us to believe as he or she desires.

3. Attempting an impossible synthesis (17:39-41)

In compliance with the instructions of the priest, they took up the outward form of worshipping God while retaining their own gods. Matthew Henry says they 'worshipped the God of

Israel for fear and their own idols for love'.[1] Alexander Maclaren offers this observation: 'They gave God formal worship, but they gave the others more active service.'[2]

God is never pleased with divided allegiance. In his Sermon on the Mount, the Lord Jesus said to his hearers, 'No one can serve two masters; for either he will hate the one and love the other, or else he will be loyal to the one and despise the other. You cannot serve God and mammon' (Matt. 6:24).

This part of 2 Kings must have touched a nerve with its original readers. They were in captivity because they had made the very same mistake as those who had replaced them in the land. They had ignored the first of the Ten Commandments: 'You shall have no other gods before me' (Exod. 20:3). They had also ignored the Second Commandment: 'You shall not make for yourself a carved image' (Exod. 20:4). They had assured themselves that it was possible to have it both ways, to worship God and their idols, but their captivity proved how dreadfully they had miscalculated.

The fact that they were now in captivity in no way released them from their obligations to God. They were still to live according to his commandments and to worship and serve him only. But there in their new land, they were again facing the temptation to blend the worship of God with the religious practices of their captors.

The book of Daniel deals with this very same issue. Daniel and his friends were taken captive from Judah by the Babylonians. In Babylon they faced tremendous pressure to practise Babylonian religion alongside their own religion. But these men, by the grace of God, showed time after time that their allegiance was to Jerusalem even though they themselves were in Babylon.

Our culture coaxes us to attempt this blending as well. It constantly tells us that we can have it both ways, that we can be true to God and still think and act like those around us. But it is impossible to embrace mutually exclusive options. We cannot be true to God and at the same time embrace thoughts and actions that are opposed to him.

Many these days regard these matters as nothing more than splitting hairs. They love imprecision in religion, but God loves precision. He is not happy with anything and everything that goes under the name of religion. Like it or not, it is possible to be wrong in religion, so wrong that we can even end up in eternal destruction. Let us be on guard, then, against compartmentalizing God, accepting wrong authority and the temptation to synthesize the worship of God with something else.

26.
Hezekiah: a pattern for devoted and faithful living

Please read 2 Kings 18:1-8

As we have noted, the book of 2 Kings falls quite naturally into three major parts. Chapters 1-10 deal primarily with events in the northern kingdom of Israel. Chapters 11-17 alternate between events in both Israel and Judah. Chapters 18-25 deal with events in Judah. We have now come to the third of these divisions. By this point Israel has gone into captivity. Only Judah remains, and in these closing chapters the author focuses our attention on the 136 years before she too went into exile.

Judah was able to outlast her sister kingdom for so many years because from time to time God graciously gave her good kings who led her back to him. Hezekiah was one such king. We look now at his life, and we do so, not because of some quaint interest in ancient history, but rather because we find in him a pattern for our own lives. Hezekiah shows us how we ourselves ought to live. He is a pattern for a devoted and faithful life.

We might say that Hezekiah lived his life on three levels. In other words, his spiritual life may be compared to a building consisting of three storeys.

1. His destruction of idols (18:4)

The kingdom of Judah was in a state of rapid spiritual decay when Hezekiah came to the throne. His father Ahaz had made a radical break with God. In addition to worshipping idols, Ahaz had actually locked the temple of God and destroyed all its sacred articles (2 Chr. 28:1-4,22-25). Matthew Henry summarizes Ahaz's reign in this way: '... a deluge of idolatry had overspread the land.'[1]

Hezekiah began his reign by addressing the vast legacy of idolatry from his father. He removed all the high places (elevated places which were used for the worship of idols) and destroyed all the images. He also destroyed the bronze serpent which Moses had made. This serpent had been given by God to the nation of Israel as the means of healing the people from poisonous snake-bites (Num. 21:5-9). The serpent was put on a pole in the midst of the camp, and all the stricken Israelites had to do for healing was look towards that bronze serpent. It was, of course, a marvellous anticipation of the coming Christ who was to be lifted up on the cross for the spiritual healing of all sinners who look to him in faith (John 3:14-15). But the people of Judah had taken to calling it **'Nehushtan'**, that is, 'Bronze Thing', and had been using it in a way never intended or commanded by God — that is, as an object of worship. Hezekiah, seeing the evil of this, destroyed it.

A godly life cannot be built on the foundation of idolatry. All of us are idolaters by nature. We come into this world with an innate opposition to God and with the readiness to give to other things the allegiance and devotion that belong to God. Christians have, by the grace of God, been made different. They have 'turned to God from idols to serve the living and true God' (1 Thess. 1:9).

Although as Christians we have decisively broken with idolatry, it is possible for idolatry to creep back into our lives for a time. We are inclined to associate idolatry with material things. Because we do not actually see people falling down and worshipping physical objects, we may be inclined to think idolatry is a thing of the past. The truth is that we are guilty of it whenever we give something, such as a pleasure or a possession, the allegiance that belongs to God alone. To the extent that we allow ourselves to go after idols, we diminish ourselves spiritually.

2. His trust in the Lord (18:5)

A second foundational aspect of Hezekiah's spiritual life, or the second storey in his spiritual house, is expressed in these words: **'He trusted in the Lord God of Israel…'** Trust in the Lord was the wellspring of Hezekiah's devotion. This means he believed in God's revelation without reservation or doubting. He believed that God had indeed granted revelation of his truth to the nation of Judah, and that revelation provided the basis for the well-being of the kingdom.

Faith is, of course, the instrument which God uses to bring us into his kingdom. It has always been so. Some think that people in Old Testament times were saved in a different way from those in the New Testament era. More specifically, they think the Old Testament saints were saved by keeping the law, while we are saved by faith. But the Bible is uniform in its teaching on this matter, and salvation has always been by grace through faith. All the saints of all ages are saved by God enabling them to believe the truth about their sins, to see the condemnation that was awaiting them and to believe in the salvation that Christ alone has provided. The difference between the Old and New Testament eras is that people in the former were saved as they looked forward in faith to the Christ who was to come, while we look backward in faith to the Christ who has come.

The Christian does not trust God for salvation only to cease trusting him later. Trusting God becomes the pattern of his life. He depends on the teachings of God's Word. He tenaciously clings to its promises. He heeds its warnings. He obeys its commandments. He draws spiritual lessons from its heroes as well as from its villains. The true Christian cannot help but view the whole of reality through the lens of God's Word.

His perseverance (18:6)

A third important feature of, or level in, Hezekiah's spiritual life is stated in these words: **'He held fast to the Lord.'** Hezekiah's attachment to the Lord was so deeply seated in his heart that it remained constant and steadfast. It did not vary with his circumstances, no matter how difficult they were.

Alexander Maclaren makes an interesting comment on this facet of Hezekiah's spirituality. He says, 'The metaphor of cleaving implies proximity and union; the metaphor of following implies distance which is being diminished.'[2] Maclaren goes on to say, 'It is an incongruous combination of ideas, by its very incongruity and paradoxical form suggesting a profound truth ... that in all the conscious union and tenacious adherence to God which makes the Christian life, there is ever, also, a sense of distance which kindles aspiration and leads to the effort after continual progress. However close we may be to God, it is always possible to press closer. However full may be the union, it may always be made fuller; and the cleaving spirit will always be longing for a closer contact and a more blessed sense of being in touch with God.'[3]

This feature of Hezekiah's devotion is true for all children of God. God's people are not perfect in this life. They sometimes sin grievously, but the general tenor of their lives is one of holding fast to God. It is the very nature of faith to do so. The Lord Jesus himself says, 'If you abide in my word, you are my disciples indeed' (John 8:31). Those who do not hold fast to the Lord only give evidence that they never really knew him (1 John 2:19).

Hezekiah's clinging to the Lord manifested itself in his obedience to the Lord. This is first stated in negative fashion: **'He did not depart from following him.'** It is then stated positively: he **'kept his commandments, which the LORD had commanded Moses'** (18:6). For a more complete picture of the thoroughness with which Hezekiah obeyed the Lord, we can turn to 2 Chronicles 29:1 – 31:21. There we find him, among other things, cleansing the temple, restoring temple worship and keeping the Passover.

The example of Hezekiah

What a rebuke the account of Hezekiah was to the original readers of 2 Kings! They were in captivity because they had not renounced their idols, had not put their trust in the Lord and had not persevered in faithfulness to him.

What a model Hezekiah is for us in spiritual things! Here was a man who renounced idolatry, trusted the Lord and held fast to him. We are called to do the same, and we may be sure that our holding fast will be manifested in the very same ways as we refrain from those things the Lord forbids and do those things he commands.

We cannot leave Hezekiah without noticing that his devotion to the Lord had a twofold result. First, it made him unique among the kings of Judah (18:5). Secondly, it brought the blessing of God upon him and the nation in terms of their triumphing over their enemies.

We are to serve God out of hearts of love and without regard to blessing or reward, but we may be sure that God will never be in anyone's debt. We cannot faithfully serve God without receiving innumerable blessings from him.

We cannot look at the church today without coming to the conclusion that she does not seem to be enjoying unusual blessings from her God. That which the church calls blessing is nothing more than the result of applying certain business principles and procedures. The church flourishes today by virtue of the same approach that causes businesses to flourish. She is not flourishing because of God moving mightily in her midst.

We may ask ourselves why God is not moving mightily. Is it because we are not following the pattern set before us by Hezekiah? Is it because we still have our idols, we do not trust God to the degree we should and we are not clinging fast in terms of practical obedience?

27.
God in the hands of
an angry sinner

Please read 2 Kings 18:9-37

In 1741 Jonathan Edwards preached his famous sermon, 'Sinners in the Hands of an Angry God'. It was an absolutely riveting sermon. This passage presents us with an Assyrian official who functioned as something of a preacher. Far from glorifying God, as Edwards' sermon did, his sermon attacked God. We might say we have here the polar opposite of Edwards' sermon. Here we have God in the hands of an angry sinner.

Let's first try to fill in something of the background. It was a distressingly bad time for the nation of Judah. Assyria, which had already taken Israel captive, now comes against Judah. It may puzzle us that the author of 2 Kings again gives details of the captivity of Israel (18:9-12). Why would he break away from his discussion of the Assyrian threat to Judah to mention once more Assyria's conquest of Israel? Paul House suggests that he does so 'with the intention of demonstrating Hezekiah's awareness of the dangers inherent in opposing Assyria'. House further states, 'The passage also reminds readers that the fundamental reason Samaria fell was its spiritual rebellion, not merely its refusal to obey Assyria any longer. Therefore, Hezekiah may not disobey the Lord and survive.'[1]

King Sennacherib of Assyria had already seized Judah's **'fortified cities'** (18:13). Hezekiah tried to pacify him by paying a heavy tribute (18:14-16), but this did not stop him sending his army, under the leadership of three officials, to the city of Jerusalem (18:17). These officials were the Tartan (Commander in Chief), the Rabsaris (Chief Officer) and the Rabshakeh (Chief of Staff).

Hezekiah sent a delegation consisting of Eliakim, Shebna and Joah to meet with these officials (18:18) at the Upper Pool, the same site at which Isaiah the prophet had years earlier confronted Hezekiah's father (Isa. 7:3).

The Assyrians immediately resorted to blustery, intimidating tactics. They evidently thought that they could, without firing so much as a single arrow, bully Hezekiah into surrender. This episode would have been of help to the captives in Babylon. They found themselves surrounded by sceptics who did not hesitate to taunt them (Ps. 137:1-3). These tactics should also be of interest to each and every child of God. We have an enemy far more dreadful than the Assyrians, namely, Satan. He commands a vast army of spiritual powers that have sworn eternal hostility towards our spiritual well-being.

We should not be surprised that Satan uses the same tactics against us that the Assyrian officers adopted with the leadership of Jerusalem. It is no surprise because the situation in 2 Kings was not merely a confrontation between the Assyrians and the city of Jerusalem. It was between Satan and the people of God. The Assyrians were merely the instruments of Satan at this particular time.

We do well to inform ourselves of Satan's tactics so that we can be on guard against them. We can divide our consideration of these tactics into two parts: the Assyrians' message to Hezekiah (18:17-25) and their message to the people of Jerusalem (18:26-37).

1. The Assyrians' message to Hezekiah (18:17-25)

The Rabshakeh spoke for the Assyrian delegation. Although Hezekiah himself was not present, the Jerusalem delegation was representing him and would report back to him. Aware of this, the Rabshakeh began by saying, '**Say now to Hezekiah ...**' (18:19).

The Rabshakeh's message to Hezekiah can also be divided into two sections. He first told the king that he was a fool to trust Egypt (18:21,23-24); then that he was a fool to trust God (18:22-25).

This passage is not without irony. The Rabshakeh was absolutely right in what he said about Egypt. Hezekiah was wrong, as the prophecy of Isaiah so clearly indicates, to look to Egypt for military assistance. The people of God were to look to him as their resource (Isa. 30:1-7). They were to trust him for deliverance from their enemies.

It was to this business of trusting God that the Rabshakeh soon turned. He had no hesitation at all in ridiculing Hezekiah for trusting God. He did so along a couple of lines.

1. A false assumption

First, he suggested that Hezekiah was not on the best of terms with God because the king had destroyed high places and altars that were used for the worship of God (18:22).

Nothing is sadder than to hear someone pronouncing on the Bible who obviously does not have a clue as to what it is about. That is essentially what we have here. The Rabshakeh could not have made a more colossal blunder. He suggested that God was not pleased with Hezekiah for tearing down these high places and altars. The truth is that God could not have been more pleased. God detested these high places and altars and insisted on centralized worship in the temple in Jerusalem. But because these high places and altars were used in the name of worshipping God, the Rabshakeh assumed that God was pleased with them. Many today think God is pleased with everything that is done in his name, but he is not. If we want to know what pleases him, we must look into his Word.

So Hezekiah was on far better terms with God than the Rabshakeh realized. Satan delights in making Christians think that God is always upset and angry with them, that there is no need to serve God because he can never be pleased with anything they do. But the Bible teaches that, while the people of God are always imperfect and unprofitable servants, the Lord is indeed pleased with them because they are clothed in the righteousness of Christ and their works are made acceptable and, as it were, a pleasing fragrance, through the redeeming work of Christ.

2. A false claim

The Rabshakeh sought to further shake Hezekiah's faith in God by suggesting that he and the Assyrian army had been led by God to come up against Jerusalem. He asked, **'Have I now come up without the LORD against this place to destroy it? The LORD said to me, "Go up against this land, and destroy it"'** (18:25).

What an easy thing it is to claim that God is behind what we ourselves want to do! How easy it is to claim his leadership when we are simply following our own desires! Many set aside the plain teachings of God's Word because those teachings cut against the grain of their desires. Some even go so far as to reject the teachings of the Word of God on the basis that God is leading them to do so! They casually toss aside Scriptures that disturb them on the ground that they are out of keeping with the spirit of the Lord Jesus. Imagine it — appealing to the Lord and our understanding of his leadership to undermine the leadership he gave the authors of Scripture!

We should rejoice that Hezekiah was not affected by the Rabshakeh's attempt to shake his faith. When Hezekiah received the report of the Rabshakeh's words, he responded by going into the house of the Lord (19:1).

The devil is still in the faith-shaking business. He would have every child of God believe he is a fool for believing in God, but the true child of God cannot abandon his faith. He discovers to his surprise that it holds him more than he holds it. The world will always pity and deride the believer, but the believer will by the grace of God persevere. He finds that he cannot help but believe.

The Assyrians' message to the people of Jerusalem (18:26-37)

Hezekiah's representatives were unnerved by the Rabshakeh's message to the king. Knowing it would have an unsettling effect upon the people standing nearby, they asked the Rabshakeh to speak in Aramaic, thereby making it impossible for the people to understand (18:26). It was a foolish request that should never have been made. It served only to call the people nearby to the Rabshakeh's attention. He quickly seized the opportunity to intimidate them.

The main theme of his message is impossible to miss. It was that the people should not listen to their king. This message, sometimes put in slightly different words, is stated four times (18:29,30,31,32).

We have, then, competing and conflicting messages in this passage. One was the message of Hezekiah, which was that they should trust in the Lord. The other was the message of the Assyrian king as stated by the Rabshakeh (18:28). The people of Judah had to determine which of the two they would believe.

The Rabshakeh was not content simply to state the message of the King of Assyria. He also gave the people of Judah reasons for accepting it.

1. An easy life

One reason was that to do so would lead to a far more pleasant and easy life (18:32). Satan still tells people to reject Christianity because it is difficult. It requires us to break with our sins and to serve the Lord Jesus Christ in a sacrificial way. No, it is not easy, but the fact that it is not easy does not mean it is wrong. If the easy way is the right way, the Lord Jesus Christ would never have come into this world to die in the place of sinners.

2. The example of other nations

Having given this reason, the Rabshakeh moved to a second reason why the people should accept his message, which was that the Assyrians had already conquered several nations, and each of these nations had its gods. No god had been able to deliver these nations. Why, therefore, should the people of Judah believe that their God could do what no other god had been able to do? (18:33-35).

The grand assumption in all this was, of course, that the God of Judah was no different from all these other gods. The people of Judah might claim superiority for their God, but to the Rabshakeh, he was no different from any other god.

Those of us who profess faith in Christ are under constant attack at this point in these days. We are told that we are wrong to claim finality for Christ. We are accused of being intolerant, dogmatic and culturally insensitive. Pluralism is the order of the day. Each religion, we are told, has its own unique contribution to make, and no one has the right to elevate one religion over another.

How shall we respond to such talk? We must make it clear that our claims for Christ do not arise from simple dogmatism on our part, but rather from the claims of Christ himself (John 14:6). And we must also show that these claims are not mere words. They are backed up by many evidences, of which the most notable is Jesus' resurrection from the dead. The one who rose from the grave never to die again is obviously no mere man. He is nothing less than what he himself claimed to be — God in human flesh.

The message for the captives in Babylon

When the book of 2 Kings finally came into the hands of the captives, the Assyrians had been replaced by the Babylonians as the dominant power. Now the captives were hearing from the Babylonians the same message that their fathers had heard from the Assyrians. This message told them that they could not trust their God. He was so displeased with them that he would never again have anything to do with them. It was a message that suggested that even if God wanted to deliver them, he did not have the power to do so. If he could not keep them from being conquered in the first place, what reason did they have to believe that he could deliver them? Their God, the Babylonians argued, had proved to be no more effective than the gods of all the other nations Babylon had conquered.

Furthermore, the Babylonian message insisted that the captives were actually better off as they were. Babylon could offer so much more than little, provincial Judah.

The circumstances of the captives were such that the message of the Babylonians must have from time to time sounded very appealing and plausible. By reading the account of the Rabshakeh the captives could, and would, be reminded that the powers of this world are always under the power of God, and that those who put the message of God above that of the world will finally be vindicated, notwithstanding their current circumstances.

28.
'Because you have prayed to me ... I have heard'

Please read 2 Kings 19:1-37

The thunderclouds of trouble were brooding over Hezekiah and the people of Judah. The mighty and ferocious Assyrian army had invaded the land and was demanding surrender. There seemed to be no good option for Hezekiah and his people. They did not possess the military strength to defeat the Assyrians, but surrender would mean being removed from their own land and having to live in Assyria (18:31-32).

Hezekiah was a man of strong faith, and while the situation looked hopeless, he knew it was not. He did not have the manpower or the weapons to mount a successful resistance against Assyria, but he did have in his arsenal another kind of weapon — a mighty weapon indeed, the weapon of prayer. In this chapter we find Hezekiah wielding that weapon. After hearing the threats of the Assyrian delegation, he urged his friend Isaiah to pray (19:3-5). God graciously responded to Isaiah's prayer by assuring the prophet that the Assyrian threat would soon pass (19:6-7).

But before it passed, there was yet more intimidation from the Assyrian leaders. A report suddenly reached these leaders that the King of Ethiopia was coming to make war against them. Knowing it would not be wise to go out and confront the Ethiopians with Hezekiah's army behind them, the Assyrians made another attempt to persuade Hezekiah to surrender quickly (19:8-13). This attempt came in the form of a letter (19:14). When Hezekiah received it, he himself went to prayer. This chapter presents us, then, with a praying prophet and a praying king, and by so doing it urges us to remember the mighty weapon of prayer and to resort to it in our times of need. The primary focus of this chapter is on the prayer of Hezekiah and the answer he received from the Lord.

Hezekiah's prayer (19:15-19)

We can learn some very important lessons about praying by examining this prayer.

1. Prayer should begin with worship and praise

Even though Hezekiah was faced with an emergency situation, he still took time to worship the Lord. He approached God in this way: **'O Lord God of Israel, the one who dwells between the cherubim ...'** (19:15). With these words he recognized both the sovereign power of God and his covenant relationship with his people. The latter is conveyed by the description of God as dwelling between the cherubim. This was a reference to the ark of the covenant, which was the central symbol of that covenant relationship.

Hezekiah proceeded to acknowledge that God alone is God, and that he made both heaven and earth (19:15). His prayer makes us think of that of the apostles when they too found themselves in a critical situation (Acts 4:24).

Hezekiah was facing a desperate situation, but he did not begin with the situation, but rather with God. In doing so, he was, however, doing a whole lot to help himself cope with the situation. By focusing on the greatness of God, he was reminding himself that God was greater than the situation and well able to handle it. The more we try to make prayer about ourselves, the more we rob ourselves of the power of prayer. Prayer is about God.

2. It should be directed to the honour of God

A second lesson we learn from Hezekiah's prayer is to direct it to the honour and glory of God (19:16-19).

Hezekiah and his people were being threatened by the Assyrian army. A lot was at stake. An Assyrian victory would mean loss of freedom, possessions and maybe even life itself.

The thing that was of greatest concern to Hezekiah, however, was that the Assyrians had attacked God himself. Sennacherib, King of Assyria, had sent words to **'reproach the living God'** (19:16). This was like a sharp stick in the eye to Hezekiah. It was true that the Assyrians had indeed defeated other nations and had completely destroyed and discredited their gods (19:17-18). But Hezekiah wanted the Assyrians and everyone else to know that the God of Judah was not just another in a long line of gods. Hezekiah was jealous for the glory of God. He wanted **'all the kingdoms of the earth'** to know that God alone is God (19:19).

God is jealous of, and zealous for, his own glory. Even the cross of Christ is about the glory of God. There God glorified, or magnified, both his justice and his grace. His justice was magnified in that God judged sin in the person of his Son. And his grace was magnified in that God provided a way for sinners to have their sins forgiven. If God is zealous for his glory, we may rest assured that he will be most apt to show himself strong on behalf of his people when they concern themselves with his glory.

How this tests and challenges us! How concerned are we for the honour of God? We lament and bemoan the wickedness of our day, but how much of this flows from a concern for the glory of God, and how much of it is from concern for what prevailing wickedness will do to our own happiness and well-being? Even pastors have much to ponder at this point. It is very easy for us to be more concerned about building a name for ourselves than we are about bringing honour to God.

3. Boldness in presenting our needs to the Lord

Hezekiah presented his petition to the Lord in these words: **'Now therefore, O LORD our God, I pray, save us ...'** (19:19). The fact that prayer is to be occupied with worship of God and with concern for his glory does not mean there is no room at all for our petitions. It means rather that our petitions are to be properly framed and properly motivated. But with those things in place we are free to bring our requests to the Lord with the confidence that he cares about us and hears us.

God's answer (19:20-34)

The Lord gave Hezekiah an answer to his prayer through the prophet Isaiah (19:20). J. Oswalt notes: 'Sennacherib has spoken to Hezekiah concerning the Lord; Hezekiah has spoken to the Lord concerning Sennacherib; now the Lord speaks to Hezekiah concerning Sennacherib. It is always this last account which matters.'[1]

The Lord's answer may be divided into three major sections.

1. A taunt

First, the Lord taunted Assyria (19:21-28). He put her on notice that no one will be allowed to blaspheme and reproach his name with impunity.

The King of Assyria was very boastful and proud. He felt very secure in his belief that the God of Judah was no different from the gods of the other nations. He believed that he could blaspheme and reproach this God without consequences and that he was not answerable to God. He did not hesitate, therefore, to go about saying, 'I ... I ... I ... I ...' (19:23-24).

But the Lord would not allow Sennacherib to get away with such blasphemy. He answered the Assyrian's 'I's with some 'I's of his own. With these 'I's the Lord made the following abundantly plain:

> He is the Creator (19:25).
> He had allowed Assyria to have success (19:25-26).
> He knew all about Assyria's hatred of him and would bring her into judgement because of it (19:27-28).

Sennacherib of Assyria has long since perished but his spirit has not. There are multitudes today who hate God and rage against him as did Sennacherib of old. They fancy that they are getting away with it, but in due time God will answer just as he did then. We may rest assured that his answer will be much the same. He is the Creator of all things, and we are, therefore, under his authority. He gives to those who hate him the very air they breathe to mock his name, but he also takes note of their mockery and hatred and will eventually bring it to a screeching halt.

2. A sign

Secondly, the Lord gave Hezekiah a sign in the realm of nature (19:29-31). The land of Judah would be completely replenished after two full years. Judah and Jerusalem would be safe again.

3. A promise

Finally, the Lord gave Hezekiah a definite promise (19:32-34). He flatly asserted that Sennacherib would not come into the city or even shoot an arrow there. And here is the reason the Lord gave: **'For I will defend this city, to save it for my own sake and for my servant David's sake'** (19:34).

The author reports the results of this promise in verses 35-37. The first was the death of 185,000 of the Assyrian army (19:35), an event which some commentators attribute to the outbreak of some kind of epidemic. The form in which it came is not important. The key point is that this large death toll was due to the Lord's intervention on behalf of his people.

The next result was that Sennacherib withdrew from Judah (19:36). Howard F. Vos concludes that Sennacherib recognized the plague 'as a supernatural event' and withdrew in 'disgrace'.[2] Back in his homeland, Sennacherib was assassinated by two of his sons as he was engaged in worshipping the god Nisroch (19:37). The Lord had abundantly fulfilled his promise to defend Jerusalem. The army of Assyria was decimated and Sennacherib, the architect of the siege against Jerusalem, lay dead.

Encouragement for God's people

This passage contained tremendous encouragement for the captives in Babylon. Just as Hezekiah faced a daunting challenge from the Assyrians, the exiles were facing a daunting challenge in Babylon. Hezekiah's response to the challenge he faced had to come as a cheering reminder to these captives. They were not without resources in Babylon. They had with them the mighty resource of prayer. We know one of the exiles, Daniel, made consistent and effective use of that prayer (Dan.

2:17-19; 6:10-11; 9:3), and we may safely assume that many of his fellow-captives did the same.

This passage also contains encouragement for the people of God today. We so very often find ourselves like Judah of old. Our God is taunted and our faith is treated with contempt. What is the answer for the church? Is it to water down our faith so that it will be acceptable to modern-day sceptics? Is it to abandon our faith?

Our answer is found in these soul-cheering words from our God: **'Because you have prayed to me ... I have heard'** (19:20). God is always our one and only resource, and he delights to show himself strong on behalf of his people when they realize their helplessness and come to him in prayer. The world mocks our praying. It may seem such a meagre resource, but the world enormously underestimates true praying. It is powerful beyond description because the eternal God himself stands behind it and works through it.

Our great example in praying, as in every other aspect of life, is, of course, the Lord Jesus Christ. What use he made of the powerful weapon of prayer! Luke says he often withdrew into the wilderness to pray (Luke 5:16) and, on one occasion, continued all night in prayer (Luke 6:12). Because he walked in perfect communion with the Father, he was able to say, 'Father, I thank you that you have heard me. And I know that you always hear me...' (John 11:41-42).

29.
Three consoling truths

Please read 2 Kings 20:1-11

This passage comes as a shock. Hezekiah was in the midst of a life devoted to the glory of God when the prophet Isaiah told him he would soon die (20:1).

We want to believe that our lives will be free of trials and difficulties if we are generally faithful to the Lord, but here is a man whose faithfulness was about to be rewarded with an early death. How are we to explain such a thing? We shall never have the full answer in this life. We must be satisfied to know the Lord's ways are not our ways and that he uses trials and difficulties to further his purposes in our lives (Rom. 8:28).

This is a very vital and interesting passage. It casts the spotlight on certain truths that we need to see again and again.

1. God hears and answers prayer (20:1-5)

Hezekiah did a very wise thing after hearing Isaiah's shocking announcement. **'He turned his face toward the wall, and prayed to the LORD'** (20:2). Hezekiah was convinced that the Lord can, and does, work through the prayers of his people; so he prayed. What a prayer it was! As we survey it, we cannot help but note certain features.

An intense and fervent prayer

The fact that Hezekiah turned his face to the wall suggests that he did not want to be distracted by anything. He was completely focused and absorbed with praying about the crisis.

A bold prayer

It was so bold that we might be inclined to say it was lacking in reverence for God. Hezekiah did not want to die, and he made it known that he did not want to die.

He was in the prime of life and still had much to offer God in terms of faithful service. His plea to God to remember his years of faithful service (20:3) was not bragging. It was Hezekiah's way of saying that additional years of life would yield more faithful service to God. There is an element of reasoning with God here. Hezekiah was essentially asking the Lord this question: 'Why do you want to deprive yourself and your kingdom of the faithful service that I can offer?'

A properly motivated prayer

I have already alluded to Hezekiah's motivation to some degree in what I have said about his boldness. He wanted his life extended so that he could continue to serve the Lord. I would sharpen this point by saying that he prayed out of concern for the future of his nation.

S. G. DeGraaf explains this point in this way: '"In those days" must be understood to mean at the time of the Assyrian invasion. In the light of the promise recorded in II Kings 20:6, Hezekiah's illness should be placed at the beginning of this invasion. Then we can better understand his passionate prayer for recovery. Hezekiah wanted to save his people. This desire showed that the Spirit of the Mediator was in him. As a result of his sickness and recovery, his dependence upon the Lord was strengthened so that he would truly be able to serve as his people's deliverer.'[1]

In this capacity as intercessor, Hezekiah serves as only a faint picture of the Lord Jesus Christ. The author of Hebrews says of Christ, 'Therefore he is also able to save to the uttermost those who come to God through him, since he always lives to make intercession for them' (Heb. 7:25).

There is a balance for God's people to strike on the issue of death. We should not fear death, but neither should we eagerly desire it. Each Christian should have such a fervent desire to serve the Lord in this life that he is reluctant to relinquish the opportunity.

An effective prayer

Hezekiah's prayer received an immediate and merciful answer. Before Isaiah left the premises, the Lord told him to go back with the good news that Hezekiah would be healed of the malady threatening his life and that he would receive an additional fifteen years of life (20:4-6).

This creates a disturbing dilemma for students of Scripture. It gives the impression that God changes his mind, that he is whimsical and arbitrary, deciding one moment to do something and then the next moment deciding the opposite. This is a problem because of the scriptures that assert that God is unchangeable (Num. 23:19; Mal. 3:6; James 1:17).

What are we to say about this? It is true, of course, that God is sovereign and unchangeable, that he follows his plans with perfect faithfulness without darting abruptly and impulsively in first one direction and then another. When God appears to change his mind, it is, in fact, in appearance only. It was always God's plan and purpose for Hezekiah to live the additional fifteen years. But by taking him through this particular experience, the Lord was teaching his servant not to take life for granted, to lean heavily upon prayer and to understand that prayer is an indispensable part of the way in which God achieves his purpose.

We shall never fully understand prayer. But there is one truth we must grasp: God places an immense value on prayer. And while he certainly can work apart from it, he delights to work through it. Richard D. Nelson is right to say, 'Prayer remains the bedrock of daily Christian living...'[2] It is not for us to solve the mysteries of prayer. It is our responsibility to pray.

2. God works through instruments (20:7)

It is striking that after assuring Hezekiah that he would be restored to health, Isaiah proceeded to prescribe that a **'lump of figs'** should be laid on the boil that was afflicting him. If God had promised to heal Hezekiah, why was the poultice necessary? It was because God has decided to work through means.

If God knows what we need, why should we pray? Because, as we have noted, God has determined that he will make prayer the means through which he works.

If God knows all those who will finally be saved, why do we need to evangelize and do missions? Because these are the means God has selected to save those who will be saved.

What is the point of a Christian going to the doctor when he is sick? If God wants to heal him, can he not do so without doctors and medicines? Certainly, he can. But God has determined that he will do most of his healing by means of doctors, medicines and hospitals.

We should rejoice that God uses instruments. That means he can use us in the service of his kingdom.

3. God can and does perform miracles (20:8-11)

The account does not end with the promise of Hezekiah's healing. That healing in and of itself was miraculous enough. But there is also here Hezekiah's request for a sign (20:8). Isaiah offered Hezekiah a choice. Did he want the shadow on the steps to go forward or backward? Hezekiah chose the latter, saying, **'It is an easy thing for the shadow to go down ten degrees'** (20:10). John Gill says of Hezekiah's statement that the forward movement was 'an easy thing': 'That is, it was comparatively so, otherwise to go down ten degrees at once would be extraordinary and miraculous; but that was more agreeable to the nature and course of it to go forward, and so the miracle would be less apparent...'[3]

While the backward direction of the shadow was harder than the forward, it was not too hard for God. Hezekiah made the request, and the shadow moved back. We need not enter the debate of whether the miracle was with the sun or only with the shadow. The important thing is that it happened (20:11). And Hezekiah had an indisputable sign. Terence E. Fretheim writes, 'If God can delay time, the time of his [Hezekiah's] death can be delayed.'[4]

God is not shut out of his world. While he made it to operate under certain natural laws, he is able to step in and supersede or suspend those laws. The key is, of course, God's sovereign will. He performs miracles when he pleases. Some would make God's people sovereign in this area. They insist that we should have the shadow constantly dancing up and down the steps and mountains flying about. As far as they are concerned, all hospitals, nursing homes and even cemeteries could be emptied if God's people would just ascend to a higher plane of faith. But God does not do miracles all the time. While he sometimes heals, often he does not. Hezekiah springs from his sickbed, while Job languishes on his.

Others would have us believe that the miracles of the Bible never took place at all, that the accounts of them are nothing more than the products of the over-active imagination of some highly excitable people. But we must not deny the miraculous. To do so is to burn the bridge over which we ourselves must cross. The greatest miracle of them all is tersely stated by the apostle Paul in these words: 'God was in Christ' (2 Cor. 5:19). If there can be no miracles, Jesus could not have come to this earth, and he could not have risen from the grave. We must have miracles to have Jesus, and we must have Jesus in order to have forgiveness of our sins and eternal life with God in heaven.

In the final analysis, the question is not whether we believe the Bible accounts of miracles, but rather whether we believe in the God of the Bible.

30.
Hezekiah receiving visitors

Please read 2 Kings 20:12-21

Hezekiah has gone from victory to victory. The Lord has delivered him and his kingdom from the Assyrian Empire, and has delivered him from death. Hezekiah's string of victories comes to a sudden and disappointing end in the verses before us. This unhappy episode poignantly reminds us that we never in this life advance so far in spiritual things that we are beyond the possibility of sin. Even the most stalwart in faith can fail, and fail miserably. Spiritual victories, no matter how mighty and moving, do not inoculate us against failure. We must walk with the Lord each day as if it were our very first day of walking with him.

Hezekiah failed when he received a visit from Babylonian envoys. This led to another visit to Hezekiah, one from Isaiah the prophet. These two visits should lead us to spend time considering certain truths that are of the utmost importance.

A visit from the Babylonians (20:12-13)

The visit from the Babylonians ostensibly came about because of Hezekiah's illness (20:12). Learning of his recovery, the son of the King of Babylon sent him a letter and a present by the hand of some emissaries.

Hezekiah warmly welcomed them and gave them a tour. He **'showed them all the house of his treasures — the silver and gold, the spices and precious ointment, and all his armoury — all that was found among his treasures. There was nothing in his house or in all his dominion that Hezekiah did not show them'** (20:13).

Some have wondered how Hezekiah could have had such treasures so soon after paying a heavy tribute to Sennacherib (18:14-16). The most likely answer is that Hezekiah had replenished his treasures from the spoils left by the Assyrian army which had departed in such haste (19:35-36). Hezekiah also had time after the Assyrian threat was removed to receive revenue from his own citizens and from other nations (2 Chr. 32:23).

Hezekiah's warm reception of these men and his display of his treasures may look to us to be quite harmless. We might even find ourselves inclined to commend him for showing a charitable spirit, but, however innocent his action may at first appear, in fact it was far from being so. The Babylonians nurtured dreams of conquest, and what these men saw in Jerusalem was duly reported in Babylon. From that moment, Judah was added to Babylon's wish-list.

A visit from the prophet Isaiah (20:14-19)

After the Babylonians departed, Isaiah came to see Hezekiah. How the prophet knew about the visit of the Babylonians is unspecified, but it is likely that the Lord revealed it to the prophet. The same prophet who had comforted Hezekiah in the past is now called upon to rebuke him.

His penetrating questions (20:14-15)

Isaiah began his visit by posing sharp and piercing questions: **'What did these men say, and from where did they come to you? ... What have they seen in your house?'** (20:14,15). These questions must have made Hezekiah immediately aware that his entertainment of the Babylonians was not the innocent thing he had thought it to be. Isaiah's probing questions suggested something sinister and dangerous.

His sobering prophecy (20:16-18)

Hezekiah did not have long to wonder about the meaning of Isaiah's questions. After receiving the king's answers, the prophet immediately said that their visit was a chilling picture of a future day when they would return to Jerusalem. That second visit would be horribly different. Instead of sending a delegation, the King of Babylon would send his army. Instead of engaging in polite talk, the Babylonians would wage war. Instead of viewing the king's treasures, they would seize them. Instead of bidding the Jews a fond farewell, they would take them to Babylon as their captives. And Hezekiah's own descendants would serve as eunuchs in the King of Babylon's palace.

So Hezekiah had followed an ill-considered policy. He had been very naïve, assuming that his visitors were quite harmless when, in fact, they represented a future of misery and woe for his nation. Little did he realize that he had been clutching a viper to his breast!

We cannot help but set this alongside the previous account of Hezekiah's sickness. He had handled that situation admirably well, taking it to the Lord in prayer. Here he fails. Everything is going well. The Assyrian threat has been removed. Hezekiah's health has been restored. Hezekiah had handled adversity well, but he fumbles badly in prosperity. God's people often find prosperity to be a greater test than adversity.

Hezekiah's response (20:19)

Hezekiah responded to Isaiah's message by saying, **'The word of the LORD which you have spoken is good! ... Will there not be peace and truth at least in my days?'** (20:19). Commentators are divided on whether Hezekiah responded well to Isaiah's prophecy about the coming Babylonian conquest. Some suggest that he was so absorbed with his own comfort that he had no concern at all about the future of the nation. Others say he was only recognizing that the message spoken by Isaiah was God's Word and that it was irreversible. Given Hezekiah's spiritual history, we cannot think that he would be guilty of the former.

Hezekiah's lapse, significant as it was, did not cancel out the good that he did. The fact that he bowed in submission to the Word of God reveals something of the greatness of the man. The author shows us even more of that greatness by taking note of the tunnel Hezekiah built (20:20). This tunnel, approximately 1,780 feet (or 542.5 metres) long, connected the Gihon Spring east of Jerusalem with the Pool of Siloam, which was in the southern part of Jerusalem. It was a significant accomplishment because it enabled his people to bring water into the city of Jerusalem during times of siege.

After reigning so long and so effectively, Hezekiah died and was succeeded by his son Manasseh (20:21) who promptly led the nation into its darkest era.

A call to ponder certain truths

The author of 2 Kings did not relate the details of Hezekiah's reception of the Babylonian envoys as a matter of mere academic interest. He wrote as a pastor who was concerned about the spiritual welfare of his people. We can be sure, therefore, that he wanted his readers to carry away from their reading of this event certain truths. We might say the two visits Hezekiah received in this passage were intended to encourage them, and us, to spend time in the company of certain important truths.

1. The need to be discerning

What are we to learn from Hezekiah's fond treatment of the Babylonians? One thing is to be watchful and discerning. Hezekiah failed to be on guard. He did not think the Babylonians constituted a threat to his nation. They were far too impressive for that. They were kind, warm, personable, witty and charming. But behind that pleasant façade, they harboured evil designs.

We Christians know we have a great enemy in Satan, but we are not always on guard against him. Sometimes we can be incredibly naïve about his devices. The problem is that Satan doesn't come to us snarling and threatening, but rather as an 'angel of light' (2 Cor. 11:14). Satan loves to come in the form of false teachers and preachers, who, like the Babylonians, are so kind, pleasant and affable that it seems impossible for them to be his ministers. But behind the charming façade, Satan lurks.

We are called, then, not to accept at face value all teachers (1 John 4:1), no matter how pleasant and charming they are, but to set all they say beside the Word of God to see if it corresponds (Acts 17:11).

2. The need to be good stewards

Another lesson that emerges from Hezekiah's meeting with the Babylonians is to be good stewards of those things the Lord has put in our care.

Hezekiah was a steward, or a trustee. The Lord had given him the nation of Judah and, for that matter, all the treasures of which he was so very proud. As a steward it was his responsibility to hold the nation and its treasures in trust for the Lord. These things were not his. They were the Lord's and were to be used in the way the Lord wanted and for the Lord's glory. Hezekiah failed to be a good steward. By his warm welcome of the Babylonians, he put the nation at risk.

Every child of God is a steward of certain things. We are stewards of our bodies, our homes, our churches and, yes, even the truth of the gospel itself. We must take our stewardship seriously and not allow the pleasant Babylonians of our day to compromise in these vital areas.

Hezekiah's failure and our own failures should cause us to feel immense gratitude for the Lord Jesus Christ. He also was given a stewardship. The whole work of redemption was placed in his hands. The Lord Jesus Christ did not fail, but was 'faithful to him who appointed him' (Heb. 3:2).

3. The need to guard against pride

A third lesson for us to learn from Hezekiah is to guard our own hearts, especially against pride.

Hezekiah had been successful. He had survived the Assyrian threat. He had accumulated vast treasures. He had built such a name that he was known even in far-away Babylon.

The Babylonians' visit gave Hezekiah the opportunity to show off a bit. It gave him the opportunity to enjoy his own greatness. How foolish he was! His greatness and all his successes came to him solely because of the blessing of God upon his life, but Hezekiah conveniently ignored this and yielded to pride. He was at this point facing two very dangerous enemies — the one without and the one within. The one without was the Babylonian Empire. The one within was his own pride. The tragedy was that he was blissfully unaware of each.

Pride is an exceedingly dangerous thing. It poses a far greater threat to our spiritual well-being and our usefulness to God than all the false teachers Satan can produce. And it is so very prevalent that we must agree with the cartoon character, Pogo, who said, 'We have met the enemy, and he is us.'

If it weren't for pride, the devil couldn't do much with us. If we don't have pride, there is no end to what the Lord can do with us.

4. The need to submit to God's Word

A fourth lesson we learn from Hezekiah is to bow in submission to the Word of God.

We know that God's word through Isaiah proved to be true. It took a little more than a hundred years for it to come true, but come true it did. The Babylonians did indeed invade the land of Judah, devastated it and took most of its citizens into captivity.

God's Word still speaks today. It repeatedly warns believers that God will visit their disobedience with chastisement. It warns unbelievers that God will visit their rejection of the gospel with eternal destruction. God's Word often seems to be implausible, and many have no hesitation at all in turning away from it. But that Word will prove true, and those who heed it will prove wise.

31.
Two evil reigns

Please read 2 Kings 21:1-26

From the accession of Jehoash to the death of Hezekiah, the nation of Judah had enjoyed about 150 years of reigns by good kings, with the exception of the sixteen dreadful years under Ahaz.

All of that changed very dramatically with the end of the reign of the good and godly Hezekiah. He was succeeded by his son Manasseh, whose fifty-five-year reign was the longest and the most evil of any king of Judah. This was followed by the two-year reign of Manasseh's son Amon. During these fifty-seven years Judah was in a virtual free fall of apostasy and idolatry. By the time this period ended the nation was irreversibly set on the path of judgement, so much so that even the good reign of Amon's son, Josiah, could not turn back the storm of judgement gathering on the horizon.

The reign of Manasseh (21:1-16)

A student once complained to his professor that he did not deserve the low grade on his paper. The professor responded: 'I know, but this school does not have a lower grade than the one on your paper!' As we read the author's description of

Manasseh, we could very well find ourselves thinking we need lower grades than we have available. Manasseh plumbed the depths of evil in an unprecedented and particularly grievous way, and did so for a prolonged period of time.

The author's summary of Manasseh's reign revolves around two phrases. The first phrase refers to Manasseh: **'And he did evil...'** (21:2). The second concerns the Lord's response: **'And the LORD spoke...'** (21:10).

'And he did evil...' (21:1-9,16)

It is hard to imagine more depressing reading than we have in these verses. We may gather up all Manasseh's evil acts under two headings: his idolatry and his shedding of innocent blood.

Idolatry

Paul House notes seven separate religious offences that Manasseh committed:

> 1. Worshipping idols in the same manner as those nations Israel had expelled from the land;
> 2. Allowing high places to flourish again;
> 3. Reintroducing the worship of Baal and his consort Asherah;
> 4. Bowing down 'to all the starry hosts' — that is, worshipping astral deities;
> 5. Building altars to false gods in the temple of the Lord;
> 6. Practising child sacrifice;
> 7. Consulting 'mediums and spiritists'.

House concludes his treatment of the topic with these words: 'Given this summary, it is clear that Manasseh follows all the wrong role models. He imitates the detestable Canaanites,

Jeroboam I the builder of high places, Ahab the advocate of Baal-worship, Ahaz the proponent of child sacrifice, and Saul the visitor of mediums. It is hard to imagine a more damning critique.'[1]

The shedding of innocent blood

Manasseh added to this idolatry the shedding of innocent blood. The author graphically presents this aspect of his reign: **'Moreover Manasseh shed very much innocent blood, till he had filled Jerusalem from one end to another'** (21:16).

While some of Manasseh's victims may have been killed for political reasons, we assume that the vast majority were put to death for religious reasons, that is, for opposing his idolatry. The prophets of the Lord were undoubtedly his primary targets. Many think that Isaiah the prophet was one of those the author of Hebrews had in mind when he mentioned those who were 'sawn in two' (Heb. 11:37), and that his execution was ordered by Manasseh. While we do not possess much information about those whom Manasseh had killed, we can say that these killings were particularly reprehensible in the eyes of the Lord. Matthew Henry writes, 'Nothing has a louder cry, nor brings a sorer vengeance.'[2]

We must not take the author's description of Manasseh's sins to mean that he alone was to blame for the tide of wickedness that flowed through Judah. Manasseh did not take his citizens anywhere they themselves did not want to go. Idolatry and bloodshed ran at floodtide because the people willingly followed Manasseh's lead.

'And the LORD spoke...' (21:10-15)

Given the catalogue of Manasseh's sins, we are not at all surprised to read, **'And the LORD spoke by his servants the prophets...'** (21:10).

Manasseh's evil, as is the case with all evil, was done 'in the sight of the LORD' (21:2), and the Lord is not ambivalent or nonchalant about evil. His holy nature requires him to take notice of it and to judge it. He sent his prophets, therefore, with a stinging message about coming judgement. The nature of that judgement is set out in three figures.

The tingling ears

The first figure is the tingling ears (21:12). The coming judgement would be such that anyone hearing about it would find himself astonished and filled with dread and trembling.

The plumb line

The second figure is the plumb line (21:13), a device used by builders to determine if a wall is straight, consisting of a small, heavy weight attached to a cord and suspended to indicate a vertical line. Paul House writes, 'A great "plumb line" of assessment, the same one used to measure and punish Samaria, will be stretched out against Judah...'[3]

Through the prophet Amos, God told Israel that he was about to determine if their lives were straight according to his plumb line. If they were not, he declared that he would not pass by them any longer but would send judgement upon them (Amos 7:7-9).

The upturned dish

The third figure is the wiped and upturned dish (21:13). When someone wipes a dish clean and turns it upside down, he indicates by his action that he does not intend to use it for a while. With this figure God was declaring that Judah was going to be put aside for a while. Those to whom the author of 2 Kings was writing, the exiles in Babylon, knew all too well about the fulfilment of this prophecy. They were in captivity because God had set Judah aside.

We are all familiar with parents who constantly threaten their children with punishment but never carry it out. God is not like that. He does not offer empty threats. When he says that he will send judgement, judgement comes. The author of 2 Kings will yet detail for us how God fulfilled his word pronouncing judgement on the nation of Judah.

The very same God who followed through on his warnings of judgement in this passage has decreed eternal destruction for all the wicked (2 Thess. 1:8-10). Since we are all wicked by nature, it would appear that there is absolutely no hope for us. Surprisingly enough, Manasseh himself rises from the pages of Scripture to say that there is good news for wicked people — namely, there is forgiveness with God. Manasseh, the most wicked of all Judah's kings, was soundly converted after he himself had been taken captive to Babylon (2 Chr. 33:12-13). S. G. DeGraaf says of him: 'Roaring rebellion characterized him until he was subdued by grace as a proof of the power of that grace.'[4] God had used Manasseh's chains to set him free. Joseph Hall notes: '... it is better to be a Manasseh than a Joash: Joash began well, and ended ill; Manasseh began ill, and ended well.'[5]

But while we take note of Manasseh's conversion, we must bear in mind that 2 Kings does not mention it. Why is this the case? We assume that the author's purpose was to keep the focus on judgement. The readers in Babylon needed to know that their captivity was not just an accident, but was indeed the judgement of God upon them and that it was richly deserved.

The reign of Amon (21:19-26)

Manasseh was succeeded by his son Amon. The author's account of his 'short and inglorious' reign[6] consists of two major parts.

1. A summary of his evil (21:19-20)

Amon followed his father into wickedness (but never into grace). He **'did evil in the sight of the Lord, as his father Manasseh had done. So he walked in all the ways that his father had walked; and he served the idols that his father had served, and worshipped them'** (21:20-21).

In following his father, Amon failed to follow his fathers: **'He forsook the Lord God of his fathers, and did not walk in the way of the Lord'** (21:22). The 'fathers' are not specified, but the author probably had in mind all of Amon's godly predecessors and particularly David. These were men who found delight in the law of the Lord. Amon did not.

2. A description of his death (21:21-24)

Judah was spared another long reign by an evil man when Amon, after two years, was killed in his own house by his servants (21:23), who, in turn, were executed by **'the people of the land'** (21:24). Amon's son Josiah was then crowned as king, an accession which began one of Judah's best and brightest periods. Matthew Henry concludes that the people 'did justice on the traitors that had slain the king ... and did a kindness to themselves in making Josiah his son king in his stead...'[7]

The story of Manasseh and Amon must have brought sharp pain to the captives. It served as a reminder of just how wicked their nation had become and how much she deserved the captivity.

What we can learn from these two reigns

The reigns of Manasseh and Amon yield certain truths we would do well to consider:

1. God's patience in allowing Judah to plumb the depths of wickedness for fifty-seven years, during which he sent prophet after prophet to preach repentance, shows that he does not delight in sending judgement.

2. The fact that God declared that judgement would most certainly come shows that there is an end to his patience and that he is not to be trifled with. God's delays in judgement are due to his graciously giving the opportunity to repent. They do not mean that he is unwilling to judge.

3. The length of time during which the kings and the citizens of Judah had continued in sin and refused to repent was such that the readers had to acknowledge that the judgement which had come on their nation was just.

4. The fact that a good man such as Hezekiah could have a son like Manasseh shows us that grace is not a matter of heredity. Good people can have bad children. Joseph Hall says, 'We may not measure grace by means. Was it possible that Manasseh, having been trained up in the religious court of his father Hezekiah, under the eye of so holy prophets and priests, under the shadow of the temple of God, after a childhood seasoned with so gracious precepts, with so frequent exercise of devotion, should run thus wild into all heathenish abominations...? How vain are all outward helps without the influence of God's Spirit, and that Spirit that breathes where he listeth!'[8] The same author later writes, 'Manasseh was religiously bred under Hezekiah, Josiah

was mis-nurtured under Amon; and yet Manasseh runs into absurd idolatries. Josiah is holy and devout. The Spirit of God breathes freely; not confining itself to times, or means.'[9]

5. Manasseh's eventual conversion to the Lord shows us that no one is too sinful for God to save. The devil would have us believe that some are too bad to be saved and some are too good to need salvation. Neither is the case. If Manasseh could be forgiven, anyone can. But we must not think that those who are better than Manasseh do not need to be saved. We are all by nature sinners, and we all must have God's forgiveness. One sin disqualifies us from fellowship with a holy God just as much as a thousand.

6. All that Judah had suffered over so many years at the hands of these two evil kings must undoubtedly have made the people long for the coming of that king who would do righteousness and, in so doing, ensure that his people would not suffer, but prosper.

32.
Josiah and 'the Book of the Law'

Please read 2 Kings 22:1-20

The years of Josiah's reign in Judah constituted, in the words of Paul House, 'a glittering bright spot in the nation's tragic slide to destruction'.[1]

Josiah's name is synonymous with reformation. He came to the throne after his father Amon had led the nation into the most revolting idolatry imaginable (21:19-26), and heroically led his people to repudiate their idols and submit to the Lord and his law.

The author begins his account of Josiah by noting the age at which he began to reign, the length of his reign and his mother's name (22:1). He then proceeds to apply to Josiah the formula that he used with the other good kings of Judah, saying that he did **'what was right in the sight of the LORD'** (22:2; cf. 1 Kings 15:11; 22:43; 2 Kings 12:2; 14:3; 15:3; 18:3). But the author also awards to Josiah the same description that he had previously applied only to Asa and Hezekiah — namely, that Josiah **'walked in the ways of his father David'** (cf. 1 Kings 15:11; 2 Kings 18:3).

The author goes even further in Josiah's case, adding these words: **'He did not turn aside to the right hand or to the left.'** C. F. Keil notes that this comment is squarely based on

the book of Deuteronomy (Deut. 5:32; 17:11,20; 28:14) and
that it 'expresses an unwavering adherence to the law of the
Lord'.[2]

Since Josiah could not have received training in godliness
from his idolatrous father, it is reasonable to suppose that his
mother must have led him in the ways of the Lord.

The book discovered and read (22:3-10)

Josiah's reformation appears to have proceeded slowly at first.
The fact that he, like his predecessor Joash (12:1-16), commanded that the temple should be repaired indicates that he
was on the path to removing idolatry and centralizing worship
in the temple. We should not be surprised that the temple was
in need of renovation. It always fell into disuse and disrepair
in times of rampant idolatry.

In the process of repairing the temple, the king sent Shaphan
the scribe to Hilkiah the high priest with instructions about
paying the workers (22:3-8). Hilkiah seized this opportunity
to say, **'I have found the Book of the Law in the house of
the Lord'** (22:8).

This announcement led to four readings: the first by Shaphan
himself (22:8); the second when he read it to the king (22:10);
the third in the presence of Huldah the prophetess (implied in
22:14); and the fourth when the king read it to the people
(23:2).

What was this 'Book of the Law'? In all likelihood, it was
the book of Deuteronomy. We cannot say how long the nation
had been deprived of the message of this book, but we can say
that during that time the nation was missing a most important
and vital message. Deuteronomy stresses the importance of
obedience to God. It tells of the blessings that God bestows
upon an obedient people and the devastating judgement he
sends upon those who refuse to obey.

We may wonder how Josiah could have lived righteously (22:2) without possessing this book. In all probability he was able to do so on the basis of what he had been told about the law of God by godly people.

The message of the book received (22:11-20)

The king tears his clothes (22:11)

After Hilkiah the priest found the book of the Law, Shaphan the scribe carried it to Josiah and read it to him (22:10).

The king could have said something like this: 'There's no reason for us to be concerned. This is a very old book. It is outdated. It has no relevance or application for us.' Or he might have said something along these lines: 'These are modern and sophisticated times. No one believes like that any more.' Yes, Josiah could have said such things, but he did not. Instead, '**... he tore his clothes**' (22:11). By doing so the king outwardly demonstrated what was taking place inwardly. He tore his clothes because his heart was torn with sorrow and grief over the failure of his nation to adhere to what was written in this book.

The king seeks an explanation (22:12-20)

Josiah then gave this order to Shaphan: '**Go, enquire of the Lord for me, for the people and for all Judah, concerning the words of this book that has been found; for great is the wrath of the Lord that is aroused against us, because our fathers have not obeyed the words of this book, to do according to all that is written concerning us**' (22:13).

Shaphan complied with this command by going to a prophetess named Huldah (22:14), who responded to the king's enquiry with a twofold message.

Disaster (22:15-17)

In the first place, regarding the nation as a whole, the prophetess indicated that the warnings of God's judgement contained in Deuteronomy would indeed be carried out against Judah because of the nation's idolatry (22:16-17).

Delay (22:18-20)

The second part of Huldah's message indicated that the judgement would not come during Josiah's day (22:18-20). In saying this, the prophetess noted that the king had received the Word of God with a tender heart and had humbled himself before the Lord (22:19).

A tender heart is one that is soft rather than hard. It is a heart which is capable of receiving an impression. If a seal or stamp is pressed against a stone, no impression is left, but if it is pressed against soft wax an indelible impression remains. Josiah's heart had been like soft wax when the book of Deuteronomy was pressed against it.

What this account has to say to us

The author's account of Josiah speaks to us at three major points.

1. The need to prize the Word of God

We may very well find ourselves marvelling as we read this account. How could the people of Judah have lost the very Word on which their nation was founded and by which it was framed?

The answer is, of course, that the nation had shifted from its foundation. It had forsaken God and his covenant and had embraced worthless idols. When a nation or an individual begins to move away from God, the Bible becomes a source of irritation. The Bible is the bulwark against false religion and idolatry. Those who want to promote the false must of necessity dispense with the true. We can well imagine, therefore, the idolatrous kings who preceded Josiah making a concentrated effort to destroy every copy of the Word of God.

It's easy enough for us to see the problem that existed in those days. The kings and the people of Judah themselves did not properly prize the Word of God. They were anxious to destroy it. It is much more difficult for us to see our own failures to prize the Bible as we should.

Have you pondered recently how very blessed we are to have Scripture? It is impossible to calculate the benefits that have flowed to us from this treasure. Its principles have founded nations. Its teachings have inspired history's greatest leaders. Countless missionaries have gone to foreign lands and ennobled the lives of those citizens because of the Bible. Vast numbers of hospitals and aid agencies have been founded because of the Bible. Countless institutions of learning have been launched because of the Bible. We have seen developments that have already had a monumental impact on history. Computer technology and the worldwide web, space travel and medical breakthroughs are just a few. But none of them will ever match the Bible in terms of the good achieved.

But we must prize the Bible most of all because of the spiritual benefits it bestows. How many millions of souls have been liberated by its message of salvation from sin and been brought into right standing before God through the work of the Lord Jesus Christ! How many aching hearts have been comforted by its promises!

In the light of the many benefits bestowed by the Bible, one would think that nothing would be more prized, but, alas, such is not the case. Even God's people seem often to take Scripture for granted and to neglect it. In his book, *A Passion for Faithfulness*, J. I. Packer shares with his readers a riveting account of the Puritan Richard Rogers calling an audience to value the Word of God more highly:

> Mr. Rogers was ... on the subject of ... the Scriptures. And ... he falls into an expostulation with the people about their neglect of the Bible ... he personates God to the people, telling them, 'Well, I have trusted you so long with my Bible; you have slighted it, it lies in such and such houses all covered with dust and cobwebs; you care not to listen to it. Do you use my Bible so? Well, you shall have my Bible no longer.' And he takes up the Bible from his cushion, and seemed as if he were going away with it and carrying it from them; but immediately turns again and personates the people of God, falls down on his knees, cries and pleads most earnestly, 'Lord, whatever thou dost to us, take not thy Bible from us; kill our children, burn our houses, destroy our goods; only spare us thy Bible, only take not away thy Bible.' And then he personates God again to the people: 'Say you so? Well, I will try you a while longer; and here is my Bible for you. I will see how you will use it, whether you will love it more ... observe it more ... practise it more, and live more according to it.' By these actions ... he put all the congregation into so strange a posture that ... the place was a mere Bochim, the people generally ... deluged with their own tears; and ... he himself, when he got out was fain to hang a quarter of an hour upon the neck of his horse weeping before he had power to mount; so strange an

impression was there upon him, and generally upon the people, upon having been expostulated with for the neglect of the Bible.[3]

There is more than one way to lose the Bible. We have Bibles everywhere. There does not appear to be much chance of our losing it in the way that it was lost in Josiah's day. But we can lose it in another way. We can lose its message even while we hold it in our hands.

There are many signs that this is happening. We have the Bible, but we are ignoring large portions of it. We tend to look right past those passages that talk about sin, holiness, repentance and coming judgement. There is even an increasing tendency to disregard the Bible's message about the cross of Christ being the only possible way of salvation. We are much more comfortable looking for passages that help us cope with the here and now.

The prophet Amos warned about a famine of hearing the Word of God (Amos 8:11). Such a famine exists today.

2. The need to respond appropriately to the Word of God

Josiah's eager response to the Book of the Law reflects how we are to respond to the message of God's Word. The epistle of James tells us that we are to 'receive with meekness the planted word' (James 1:21). That word 'receive' means we are to give a warm and inviting welcome to the message of God's Word. It is the same word that Luke used to describe the Bereans' response to the Word: '... they received the word with all readiness' (Acts 17:11). Paul employed the same word to describe the response of the Thessalonians to God's Word: '... you welcomed it not as the word of men, but as it is in truth, the word of God, which also effectively works in you who believe' (1 Thess. 2:13).

The life of Abraham provides us with a wonderful example of responding appropriately to the Word of God. Realizing that the three visitors who came to him were from heaven itself and brought a vital message for him, Abraham 'ran from the tent door to meet them, and bowed himself to the ground' (Gen. 18:2). Furthermore, he pleaded with them not to pass by but to allow their feet to be washed and a meal to be prepared for them (Gen. 18:3-5). After they sat down Abraham 'hurried' to tell his wife Sarah to prepare cakes, then 'ran' to the herd to get a calf and 'hastened' to prepare it (Gen. 18:6-8).

We may compare Abraham with the religious leaders with whom Jesus dealt. Were they pleading with him not to pass them by? Were they hastening to make preparations to encourage him to stay? Hardly! This caused Jesus to confront them with these stern words: 'But now you seek to kill me, a man who has told you the truth which I heard from God. Abraham did not do this' (John 8:40). While Abraham was very receptive to the truth of God, those religious leaders had no time for it at all.

How do we respond to the Word of God? Do we give it a sympathetic hearing? Do we quickly respond to its commands? Do we bring tender hearts to the Word of God? Do we humble ourselves before the God of the Word? Have we come to the place where we can heartily join with the translator who prefaced his 1734 edition of the Bible with this couplet:

'Thy whole self apply to the text;
The whole thing apply to thy self'?[4]

3. The need to trust God to preserve his Word

This passage suggests that the nation of Judah was left with only one copy of this particular portion of the Word of God. It might seem that God's Word was hanging by such a slender thread that it could have snapped at any time. If we choose to liken that book to a thread, we need not think it was slender or about to snap. If it was a thread, it was an unbreakable one. God himself ensured that it would not break. God has always taken care of his Word, and he always will.

The *Cambridge History of the Bible* relates the time when the Roman emperor Diocletian issued a decree to destroy the Scriptures: '... an imperial letter was everywhere promulgated, ordering the razing of the churches to the ground and the destruction by fire of the Scriptures, and proclaiming that those who held high positions would lose all civil rights, while those in households, if they persisted in their profession of Christianity, would be deprived of their liberty.' What became of Diocletian's decree? Consider this: twenty-five years later, the emperor Constantine ordered that fifty copies of the Scriptures be prepared at the expense of the Roman government.[5]

The French sceptic Voltaire, who died in 1778, predicted that Christianity and the Bible would be non-existent in one hundred years. Only fifty years after his prediction, the Geneva Bible Society used his press to produce Bibles and his house to store them.[6]

In the light of such things, Sydney Collett observed: 'We might as well put our shoulder to the burning wheel of the sun, and try to stop it on its flaming course, as attempt to stop the circulation of the Bible.'[7] The Bible has withstood the attacks of time, and it will continue to do so. God's Word is settled for ever in heaven (Ps. 119:89). Because of this, we can say to all the sceptics, 'God's Word is not going away. Get used to it and come to terms with it!'

We may conclude that the original readers of 2 Kings, captive in Babylon, would have needed no assistance in applying the discovery of the Book of the Law to themselves. They must have bowed in repentance as they considered how they had failed to prize the Word of God or to respond appropriately to it. They must also have found themselves rejoicing in the knowledge that the Word of God will never finally be destroyed. That Word now gave them hope for the future. What a delight it was for them to realize that it was a sure word!

33.
Josiah's reformation

Please read 2 Kings 23:1-30

The book of James warns about the danger of being a hearer and not a doer of the Word of God (James 1:22). King Josiah serves as a shining example of one who was not content to be only a hearer of the Word of God.

After hearing the long-lost book of Deuteronomy and trembling at its message (22:11-13), Josiah set the nation of Judah on a course of sweeping reform. He did so even though the prophetess Huldah had assured him that God had irreversibly pronounced judgement upon the nation (22:14-20). Josiah understood that the Lord has the right to be served even if serving him doesn't bring the benefit we may desire (in his case, the lifting of the sentence of judgement). Richard Nelson notes: 'Genuine faith transcends any desire for gain.'[1]

Josiah's devotion to the Lord was of such a nature that the author of 2 Kings awarded him this accolade: **'Now before him there was no king like him, who turned to the LORD with all his heart, with all his soul, and with all his might, according to all the Law of Moses; nor after him did any arise like him'** (23:25).

Josiah's reformation of Judah leads us to three major emphases: its sweeping nature, the element missing from it and its ultimate ineffectiveness.

The sweeping nature of the reformation (23:1-25)

Josiah carried out his reforming activities, not only in his own
kingdom of Judah (23:1-14, 21-24), but also at Bethel and in
other cities (23:15-20).

The reformation in Judah

The reformation in Judah consisted of four major elements.

1. A convening

First, Josiah convened the leaders and the people (23:1-2).

Manasseh had been guilty of leading the nation into idolatry, but he didn't lead the people anywhere they themselves
didn't want to go. Idolatry and bloodshed flourished in Judah
because the people eagerly followed Manasseh's lead. The
religious leaders were especially worthy of blame for not re-
sisting Manasseh's efforts. It was fitting, therefore, for both
the people and the leaders to hear the curses of Deuteronomy.

2. A commitment

Secondly, Josiah publicly committed himself and the nation to
the Lord (23:3).

Josiah didn't attempt to lead the people where he was not
willing to go himself. As he stood by the pillar in the temple
(evidently a place signifying authority), he made a covenant to
walk after the Lord and to keep his commandments. We are
not left to determine what walking after the Lord means. It
means keeping God's commands.

The plural 'their' at the end of this verse indicates that Josiah
was committing not only himself but the whole nation to a

new course of obedience, an obedience that would come from the heart. Josiah could not, as we shall have occasion to note, cause the people to serve God from their hearts, but he could certainly do much to encourage them in that direction.

3. A cleansing

The third aspect of Josiah's reformation in Judah consisted of cleansing the land (23:4-8).

This cleansing featured six major areas:

1. The vessels made for false gods were carried out of the temple and burned (23:4).

2. The idolatrous priests were removed (23:5).

3. The grove (**'the wooden image'**, NKJV) was destroyed (23:6). This is a reference to a lewd image of the female figure carved from a wooden pole. It was worshipped as a goddess of fertility. This was brought to the brook Kidron. The Kidron valley begins north of Jerusalem, passes the temple and the Mount of Olives and ends in the Dead Sea. Most of the year it is a dry riverbed, but in the rainy season it becomes a torrent. It was the city's rubbish dump because the garbage left there would in the rainy season be completely swept away to the Dead Sea. Kidron represented, therefore, a total removal or complete clean-up.

4. The practice of **'sacred'** prostitution was ended (23:7). The house where male prostitutes carried on their business was destroyed.

5. The high places were destroyed (23:8).

6. Mediums, spiritists and **'household gods'** were removed (23:24). The latter were probably used in the practice of divination and were, therefore, of one cloth

with the mediums and spiritists. By removing all these, Josiah was eliminating anything that competed with the Word of God and thus making it clear that the people were to look to that Word alone for guidance and direction.

4. An observance

The final aspect of Josiah's reformation consisted of observing the Passover (23:21-23). This was the feast that God gave to the people of Israel to commemorate their deliverance from bondage in Egypt (Exod. 12:1-28). It is not surprising that the Passover had not been observed. The people of Judah did not want to be reminded of what God had done for them. They were too much in love with their idols for that.

The reformation in Bethel

Having completed the reformation in Judah, Josiah turned his attention north to Bethel and beyond (23:15-20). Bethel had been the centre of the false religion established by Jeroboam when Solomon's kingdom was divided in two (1 Kings 12:25-33).

Josiah's reformation here consisted of destroying the altar and the high place erected by Jeroboam (23:15) and burning the bones of the priests of Jeroboam's religion (23:16-17). In doing the latter, Josiah made sure that he left undisturbed the bones of the prophet who had pronounced judgement on Jeroboam's religion as well as the bones of the old prophet from Bethel who had seconded the prophecy (1 Kings 13:1-34). The former had cried out against Jeroboam's altar: 'O altar, altar! Thus says the LORD: "Behold, a child, Josiah by name, shall be born to the house of David; and on you he shall sacrifice the priests of the high places who burn incense on you, and men's bones shall be burned on you" ' (1 Kings 13:2). It took 300 years for that prophecy to be fulfilled, but fulfilled it was! God's Word will finally prove true no matter how implausible it seems or how long it takes.

We cannot leave the many details of Josiah's extensive reformation without noting that they were carried out in accordance with the teachings of the laws of God (23:25).

The missing element

Although the details of Josiah's reformation are quite impressive, we cannot help but think that something is missing. If we read this chapter closely, we will find the author of 2 Kings confirming this. His emphasis is entirely on Josiah. Note the following phrases: **'the king sent'** (23:1), **'the king stood'** (23:3), **'the king commanded'** (23:4,21).

In his commentary on 2 Chronicles, Michael Wilcock notes that the accounts of previous reforms in Judah included such phrases as 'all the cities of Judah', 'all Judah', 'many people', 'whole assembly', 'great numbers', 'all Israel' (2 Chr. 19:4; 20:4,13,18; 30:6 – 31:1). Then he adds: 'But when we come to the story of Josiah, the references to God's people are strangely different. "They broke down the altars of the Baals in his presence" (34:4); and one wonders whether they would have done it had he not been there to see that it was done, because as the tale proceeds one begins to realize how little they wanted to be involved. Any sense of a corporate unity of purpose is conspicuously missing.'[2]

We might say Josiah's reformation came from his own heart but it never really touched the hearts of his people. This serves as a sharp reminder of how very easy it is to have the mere outward form of religion without really having the nub of the matter. This was the problem with the Pharisees during Jesus' ministry. They drew near to God with their lips while their hearts were far from him (Mark 7:6). Judas Iscariot, one of Jesus' twelve disciples, had the same problem.

The ultimate ineffectiveness of the reformation (23:26-30)

As we read the details of Josiah's reformation, we might also expect to read that it caused God to lift the sentence of judgement he had pronounced on Judah. It didn't. After Josiah was killed in battle (23:28-30), Judah and her kings went right back to their wickedness, and judgement finally fell.

Why did Josiah's reformation not succeed in getting God's judgement lifted? Part of the explanation may lie in what we have just noted — that is, the inadequate response of the people. But even a better response would not have reversed God's decree of judgement (23:26-27). Years and years of idolatry and refusal to repent cried out for judgement.

The failure of Josiah's reformation to genuinely touch the hearts of his people and to lift God's judgement must certainly compel us to think of the Lord Jesus Christ. He has done for all his people what Josiah could not do. The Lord Jesus has changed the hearts of his people in such a way that they love him and his commandments, and they desire to serve him. And through his redeeming work on Calvary's cross, he has removed for ever the threat of God's judgement. On that cross, God's judgement fell on Christ and, in doing so, exhausted itself. There is now no judgement remaining for those who know Christ.

34.
Judgement and hope

Please read 2 Kings 23:31 – 25:30

136 years after Israel was taken captive by the Assyrians (17:5-41), Judah experienced the same fate at the hands of the Babylonians.

Josiah was the last good king Judah had. After he was killed in battle (23:28-29), four kings came to the throne, three of whom were his sons, but the phrase, 'Like father, like son,' certainly did not apply in their cases.

The first of these four kings, Jehoahaz, a son of Josiah, reigned for only three months before he was taken captive to Egypt, where he died (23:31-34). We focus on the reigns of the last three of these four kings. During their reigns, the long-foretold Babylonian invasion came to pass. It came as God's judgement upon Judah because of her sins.

This judgement came in the form of three instalments. The account would make depressing reading indeed if the book of 2 Kings ended with these three instalments of judgement. Happily, it does not. After its description of the judgement that fell on Judah, it closes with a note of hope.

The first instalment of judgement (23:35 – 24:7)

After the brief reign of Jehoahaz, another son of Josiah, named Jehoiakim, came to the throne. One of the most notable things about this godless man is recorded for us in the prophecy of Jeremiah. The prophet had his scribe, Baruch, write a scroll consisting of 'all the words of the LORD which he had spoken to him' (Jer. 36:4). This scroll came in due course to be read to the king (Jer. 36:20-21). Jehoiakim responded by cutting the scroll into shreds and throwing it into the fire (Jer. 36:22-23). The astonishing thing to Jeremiah was that the king and his servants 'were not afraid, nor did they tear their garments' (Jer. 36:24). We cannot help but compare Jehoiakim's response to that of his father Josiah when the book of God's law was read to him (22:11-13).

The storm clouds of judgement were gathering over Judah throughout Jehoiakim's eleven-year reign. He started out paying tribute to the Egyptians, but it was not long before the Babylonians had driven the Egyptians off the stage of world influence (24:7). When the Babylonians came to prominence, Jehoiakim began paying tribute to them. He continued to do so for a period of three years. When he rebelled, Nebuchadnezzar, King of Babylon, responded by sending raiding parties against Judah.

The second instalment of judgement (24:8-16)

After Jehoiakim died his son, Jehoiachin, began his three-month reign. It was at this time that Nebuchadnezzar laid siege to the city of Jerusalem and Jehoiachin was forced to surrender.

The Babylonians took the following into captivity: the king and his family (24:12,14), the princes and officers (24:12,14), the military men and the craftsmen (24:14). In addition the

Babylonians carried off all the treasures of the temple as well as of the king's house (24:13).

All this amounted to a partial and preliminary captivity. There was, as we shall see, more to come.

The final instalment of judgement (24:17 – 25:26)

The reign and capture of Zedekiah (24:17 – 25:7)

After carrying most of Judah's leaders into captivity, Nebuchadnezzar put Zedekiah, another son of Josiah, on the throne of Judah.

If anyone ever had a clear course of conduct marked out for him it was Zedekiah. The Word of God through the prophets, and indeed common sense, made it clear that there were two priorities for him and his nation. The first was to resolutely turn from the idolatry that had brought so much grief to the nation. The second was to recognize that the Babylonians were God's instruments of judgement and submissively bow before them (Jer. 37:1 – 39:18).

Zedekiah refused to do either. He continued to do **'evil in the sight of the LORD'** (24:19), and he rebelled against the Babylonians (24:20). The author of 2 Chronicles says of Zedekiah: 'He did evil in the sight of the LORD his God, and did not humble himself before Jeremiah the prophet, who spoke from the mouth of the LORD' (2 Chr. 36:12). In other words, Zedekiah refused to live under the authority of the Word of God. He shows us how terribly hard the human heart can become. Even when men begin to experience the incredible misery created by sin, they still love it and refuse to turn from it.

Zedekiah paid a fearful price for his hardness of heart. When the Babylonians seized part of the city, he secretly fled during the night. However, the Babylonians caught him and brought him to Riblah where they killed his sons in his presence and gouged out his eyes. They then carried him captive to Babylon.

The destruction and plunder of Jerusalem (25:8-21)

The extent of Jerusalem's devastation is here presented in sickening terms. The temple, the king's house and all the houses of the rich and powerful were burned (25:9). The walls of the city were broken down (25:10). Most of the people were carried away captive, with only the poorest remaining (25:11-12).

Valuable items were also taken by the Babylonians. These included **'the bronze pillars that were in the house of the LORD, and the carts and the bronze Sea that were in the house of the LORD'** (25:13). All the other bronze items in the temple were taken away as well. The author says: **'... the bronze of all these articles was beyond measure'** (25:16).

After detailing the capture and execution of some of Jerusalem's prominent officials (25:18-21), the author sadly concludes, **'Thus Judah was carried away captive from its own land'** (25:21).

The flight of the remnant to Egypt (25:22-26)

Nebuchadnezzar appointed Gedaliah, from a prominent Jerusalem family, as governor over the people who remained in the land of Judah. Gedaliah offered wise counsel to his people, especially to the few soldiers who had returned after fleeing. If they would not cause the Babylonians any trouble, all would be well with them.

Gedaliah's term of office was brief. A band of ten men, led by someone called Ishmael, assassinated him and those present with him at Mizpah (25:25). Paul House writes, 'The reason for this murder is not altogether clear. It may be that this man of royal blood wants to claim power for himself. Jeremiah

40:13-14 states that the king of Ammon encourages Ishmael to kill Gedaliah, so regional rivalry contributes to this action.'¹

Fearing reprisal from the Babylonians, the remaining inhabitants fled to Egypt (25:26). In doing so, they disobeyed God. This act of disobedience is breathtaking. Although they had just witnessed terrible devastation as a result of their nation's refusal to live according to God's laws, they added this further act of disobedience. They did so even though God had made it explicitly clear that his people were not to be like the people of other nations but were to be set above them (Deut. 28:1). They did so in the face of clear instructions from the Lord that they were to avoid Egypt. Through Moses the Lord said of his people going to Egypt: 'You shall not return that way again' (Deut. 17:16).

The prophecy of Jeremiah gives considerable detail to this decision. The people came to him saying they wanted God to tell them 'the way in which we should walk and the thing we should do' (Jer. 42:3). After Jeremiah agreed to seek the will of the Lord for them, they said, 'Let the LORD be a true and faithful witness between us, if we do not do according to everything which the LORD your God sends us by you. Whether it is pleasing or displeasing, we will obey the voice of the LORD our God to whom we send you, that it may be well with us when we obey the voice of the LORD our God' (Jer. 42:5-6).

However, when Jeremiah returned to them with the message that they were not to go to Egypt (Jer. 42:7-22), they responded: 'As for the word that you have spoken to us in the name of the LORD, we will not listen to you! But we will certainly do whatever has gone out of our own mouth...' (Jer. 44:16-17). The remaining inhabitants had not changed. They still refused to heed the Word of God, and because of that refusal calamity came upon them in Egypt just as Jeremiah had said it would (Jer. 42:22; 44:26-30).

Lessons from judgement

2 Kings is, as we noted at the outset, the book of downfalls or captivities. The kings and the people of Israel sinned against the Lord and were taken captive. The kings and the people of Judah also sinned against the Lord and they too were taken captive. We must not treat these accounts of Israel and Judah as mere history that is of no value to us. The downfall of first Israel and then Judah teaches us the following important lessons:

1. Because God is holy, he cannot be ambivalent towards sin. His holy character requires him to judge it.

2. God does not send judgement without giving abundant warnings that it is coming. He sent the prophets Elijah, Elisha, Jonah, Amos and Hosea to Israel. He sent Obadiah, Joel, Isaiah, Micah, Nahum, Zephaniah, Habakkuk and Jeremiah to Judah.

3. God is patient and longsuffering. He sends judgement very slowly and, at first, almost imperceptibly. He gives every opportunity to repent.

4. Today's discouraged ministers can take heart from the fact that the prophets sent to Israel and Judah saw very little in the way of results, even to the point at which Isaiah cried: 'Who has believed our report? And to whom has the arm of the LORD been revealed?' (Isa. 53:1).

A note of hope (25:27-30)

The book of 2 Kings closes with a description of the treatment given by the King of Babylon to one of Judah's kings, Jehoiachin. It must seem to many to be a very unusual conclusion. Some might even be tempted to call this poor literary style. It seems as if the author did not quite know how to end so he adds this note about Jehoiachin and abruptly closes.

These concluding verses were quite deliberate on the part of the author. They were intended to provide hope for his readers. We must keep in mind that 1 and 2 Kings were written for the captives in Babylon. They were intended to answer the questions swirling around in the minds of those captives. One of those questions was this: how could God allow his own people to suffer captivity?

1 and 2 Kings answer that question. They show that it was the sins of his people that caused the captivity. The captives might be inclined to think that their situation meant that God had broken faith with his covenant people. Nothing could have been farther from the truth. The captivity, far from being a sign that God had broken faith, actually proved his faithfulness. Captivity was exactly what God had declared would happen if his people were not faithful to the covenant (Deut. 28:37,49-50,64; 30:17-18).

The author of 2 Kings also knew that the captives would be concerned about their future. God had made glorious promises to them, including the promise that the Messiah would spring from the house of David. What did the captivity mean for those promises? Could they still hope for the Messiah when the house of David appeared to be in utter ruins and perhaps on the verge of extinction? And what had become of God's promise that David's rule would last for ever? (2 Sam. 7:13).

It was this question which the author addressed in his closing verses. Yes, the people of Judah were in captivity in Babylon, but they were not to give up hope. The God who had sent them there would still fulfil his promises. The fact that Jehoiachin, a descendant of David, was nurtured and sustained in Babylon could be taken as an infallible sign that God would sustain his cause and keep his promises. The house of David was still intact, even in Babylon, and the promise of the

Messiah was still on track. The Messiah is indeed the everlasting King who will reign for ever, and in doing so, fulfils God's promise to David.

Centuries later a Jewish man and the young woman to whom he was betrothed made their way to Bethlehem, where she gave birth to the child that had been conceived in her by the Holy Spirit, and people of faith praised God as they realized that he had fulfilled his promise.

We can still rely upon this faithful God. Through the Son he gave to Mary, he has provided eternal salvation for sinners. He promises that those who repent of their sins and rest upon the saving work of Christ will have eternal life. He also solemnly warns that those who reject Christ will experience eternal destruction. Believers and unbelievers alike can depend upon God to keep his word and do as he has promised.

Notes

Introduction
1. *Holy Bible: Personal Study Bible,* Thomas Nelson Publishers, p.519.
2. As above, p.473.

Chapter 1 — A war of words
1. Ronald S. Wallace, *Readings in 2 Kings,* Wipf & Stock Publishers, p.3.
2. Matthew Henry, *Matthew Henry's Commentary,* Fleming H. Revell Publishing Co., vol. ii, p.676.
3. John MacArthur, ed., *The MacArthur Study Bible,* Word Bibles, p.1533.
4. Joseph Hall, *Contemplations on the Historical Passages of the Old and New Testament,* Soli Deo Gloria Publications, vol. ii, p.246.
5. As above, p.248.

Chapter 2 — Elijah goes home
1. Raymond B. Dillard, *Faith in the Face of Apostasy,* P & R Publishing, p.83.
2. *New Geneva Study Bible,* Thomas Nelson Publishers, p.519.

Chapter 3 — Elisha goes to work
1. Lorraine Boettner, *Studies in Theology,* The Presbyterian and Reformed Publishing Company, p.51.
2. C. F. Keil and F. Delitzsch, *Biblical Commentary on the Old Testament: The Books of the Kings,* Wm. B. Eerdmans Publishing Company, p.299.

Chapter 4 — Help for the helpless
1. Hall, *Contemplations*, vol. ii, p.265.
2. Walter Brueggemann, *Knox Preaching Guides: 2 Kings*, John Knox Press, p.14.
3. As above.
4. F. W. Krummacher, *Elisha: a Prophet for Our Times*, Kregel Publications, p.34.
5. John Gill, *Exposition of the Old and New Testaments*, The Baptist Standard Bearer, Inc., vol. ii, p.780.

Chapter 5 — An abounding supply for surpassing demands
1. Dillard, *Faith in the Face of Apostasy*, p.95.

Chapter 6 — Wonderful displays of God's mercy and power
1. Terence E. Fretheim, *First and Second Kings*, Westminster John Knox Press, p.149.
2. Dillard, *Faith in the Face of Apostasy*, p.101.

Chapter 7 — The Lord provides for the needs of his people
1. Krummacher, *Elisha*, p.70.
2. Henry, *Commentary*, vol. ii, p.731.
3. Krummacher, *Elisha*, p.76.
4. Cited in Paul House, *New American Commentary: 1,2 Kings*, Broadman and Holman Publishers, vol. viii, p.269.

Chapter 8 — Naaman in the grip of grace
1. Ronald S. Wallace, *Elijah and Elisha*, Wm. B. Eerdmans Publishing Co., p.130.
2. As above, p.131.
3. Alexander Maclaren, *Expositions of Holy Scripture*, Baker Book House, vol. ii, p.361.
4. Richard Nelson, *First and Second Kings*, John Knox Press, p.182.
5. Roger Ellsworth, *How to Live in a Dangerous World*, Evangelical Press, p.114.

Chapter 9 — Two examples of spiritual realities
1. Hall, *Contemplations*, p.291.
2. Keil, *The Books of the Kings*, p.321.

3. Fretheim, *First and Second Kings,* p.155.
4. Wallace, *Elijah and Elisha,* p.137.

Chapter 10 — Another miracle among the prophets
1. Dillard, *Faith in the Face of Apostasy,* p.124
2. Cited by Arnold Dallimore, *George Whitefield,* The Banner of Truth Trust, vol. i, p. 31.
3. As above.
4. As above.
5. As above, p.32.
6. As above.
7. Iain H. Murray, *Jonathan Edwards: A New Biography,* The Banner of Truth Trust, p.159.

Chapter 11 — Ancient messages with abiding value
1. Nelson, *First and Second Kings,* p.186.
2. Gill, *Exposition of the Old and New Testaments,* vol. ii, p.791.

Chapter 13 — Lessons from a saint and a villain
1. Cited in House, *1, 2 Kings,* p.282.
2. Nelson, *First and Second Kings,* p.193.
3. Dillard, *Faith in the Face of Apostasy,* p.143.
4. S. G. DeGraaf, *Promise and Deliverance,* Presbyterian and Reformed Publishing Company, vol. ii, p.322.

Chapter 14 — Walking Israel's way
1. DeGraaf, *Promise and Deliverance,* vol. ii, p.323.

Chapter 15 — Two abiding truths about God
1. Robert Greene Lee, *Pay-day Someday and Other Sermons,* Broadman & Holman Publishers, p.48.

Chapter 17 — Beginning again
1. Keil, *The Books of the Kings,* p.363.
2. As above.
3. David F. Wells, *No Place for Truth,* Wm. B. Eerdmans Publishing Company, p.298.

Chapter 18 — The history of Jehoash, King of Judah
1. House, *1,2 Kings,* p.304.
2. DeGraaf, *Promise and Deliverance,* vol. ii, p.335.
3. Donald J. Wiseman, *1 and 2 Kings,* Inter-Varsity Press, p.238.
4. Henry, *Commentary,* p.722.
5. Cited by House, *1, 2 Kings,* p.304.
6. Maclaren, *Expositions of Holy Scripture,* vol. iii, p. 187.
7. Hall, *Contemplations,* pp.351-2.

Chapter 19 — The tragedy of squandered opportunities
1. Maclaren, *Expositions of Holy Scripture,* vol. iii, p.26.
2. Wallace, *Elijah and Elisha,* p.163.

Chapter 20 — Amaziah and the peril of pride
1. See Roger Ellsworth, *From Glory to Ruin,* Evangelical Press, pp.244-5.

Chapter 21 — Two long reigns of prosperity and stability
1. Henry, *Commentary,* vol. ii, p.781.
2. As above.

Chapter 22 — Disintegration and decline in Israel
1. Henry, *Commentary,* vol. ii, p.784.
2. Howard F. Vos, *1, 2 Kings,* Zondervan Publishing House, p.187.

Chapter 23 — Two kings of Judah
1. 1. Henry, *Commentary,* vol. ii, p.785.
2. Wallace, *Readings in 2 Kings,* p.151.
3. DeGraaf, *Promise and Deliverance,* vol. ii, p.356.
4. Henry, *Commentary,* vol. ii, p.788.
5. As above.
6. Keil, *The Books of the Kings,* p.408.

Chapter 24 — The death of a kingdom
1. Henry, *Commentary,* vol. ii, p.785.
2. Gill, *Expositions of the Old and New Testaments,* vol. ii, p.39.

Chapter 25 — Mistakes in religion
1. Henry, *Commentary,* vol. ii, p.795.
2. Maclaren, *Expositions of Holy Scripture,* vol. iii, p.46.

Chapter 26 — Hezekiah: A pattern for devoted and faithful living
1. Henry, *Commentary*, vol. ii, p.796.
2. Maclaren, *Expositions of Holy Scripture*, vol. iii, p.51.
3. As above, pp.51-2.

Chapter 27 — God in the hands of an angry sinner
1. House, *1,2 Kings*, p.360.

Chapter 28 — 'Because you have prayed to me ... I have heard'
1. Cited in House, *1,2 Kings*, p.369.
2. Vos, *1, 2 Kings*, p.202.

Chapter 29 — Three consoling truths
1. DeGraaf, *Promise and Deliverance*, vol. ii, p.377.
2. Nelson, *First and Second Kings*, p.245.
3. Gill, *Exposition*, vol. ii, p.831.
4. Fretheim, *First and Second Kings*, p.205.

Chapter 31 — Two evil reigns
1. House, *1,2 Kings*, pp.377-8.
2. Henry, *Commentary*, vol. ii, p.817.
3. House, *1,2 Kings*, p.379.
4. DeGraaf, *Promise and Deliverance*, vol. ii, p.382.
5. Hall, *Contemplations*, vol. ii, p.407.
6. Henry, *Commentary*, vol. ii, p.817.
7. As above.
8. Hall, *Contemplations*, vol. ii, p.399.
9. As above, p.407.

Chapter 32 — Josiah and 'the Book of the Law'
1. House, *1, 2 Kings*, p.381.
2. Keil, *The Books of the Kings*, p.476.
3. J. I. Packer, *A Passion for Faithfulness*, Crossway Books, p.156.
4. Brian Harbour, *From Cover to Cover*, Broadman Press, p.57.
5. Josh McDowell, *Evidence That Demands a Verdict*, Campus Crusade for Christ, vol. i, p.20.
6. As above.
7. As above.

Chapter 33 — Josiah's reformation
1. Nelson, *First and Second Kings*, p.260.
2. Michael Wilcock, *The Bible Speaks Today: The Message of Chronicles*, Inter-Varsity Press, pp.269-70.

Chapter 34 — Judgement and hope
1. House, *1, 2 Kings*, p.400.

A wide range of excellent books on spiritual subjects is available from Evangelical Press. Please write to us for your free catalogue or contact us by e-mail.

Evangelical Press
Faverdale North Industrial Estate, Darlington, Co. Durham, DL3 0PH, England

Evangelical Press USA
P. O. Box 84, Auburn, MA 01501, USA

e-mail: sales@evangelicalpress.org

web: http://www.evangelicalpress.org